HAPPY, HEALTHY MINDS

Published in 2020 by The School of Life
First published in the USA in 2020
70 Marchmont Street, London WC1N 1AB

Copyright © The School of Life 2020
Illustrations © Lizzy Stewart
Designed and typeset by Studio Katie Kerr

Printed in Italy by Lego

The School of Life is a resource for helping us understand
ourselves, for improving our relationships, our careers and
our social lives — as well as for helping us find calm and get
more out of our leisure hours. We do this through creating
films, workshops, books and gifts.

www.theschooloflife.com

ISBN 978-1-912891-19-1

10 9 8 7 6 5 4 3 2 1

A CHILDREN'S GUIDE TO EMOTIONAL WELLBEING

HAPPY, HEALTHY MINDS

THE SCHOOL OF LIFE PRESS

Contents

Keeping Your Mind Healthy

Our minds are complicated and brilliant machines. Some people can do extraordinary things with them: work out the square root of 239,121; memorise a ten-page poem in Latin; fly an aeroplane through a thunder-storm, or cook a mushroom and spinach lasagne while helping someone to make sense of their French irregular verbs. Although our brains are only about 2% of our body's total weight, they use up to 20% of our body's energy — enough to power a lightbulb.

For much of our lives, our brain-machines run efficiently with minimal maintenance. We can feed them orange juice, biscuits, cheese straws, gulps of fresh air and the odd relaxing movie — and, on command, they'll come out with tricky spellings, facts about earthquakes and the names of all our aunts and uncles.

Like many organs in our bodies, our minds require proper attention and thought every now and then. We know we have to exercise our limbs. 200 years ago, few people thought it was a good idea to stretch their legs, lungs and hearts. If you had enough money, you could pay for someone to carry you through the streets of a town, just to make sure you wouldn't do anything as reckless as take one unnecessary step.

Nowadays, we realise that that's a fast way to an early death. Muscles wear away if we don't use them, and we need to monitor our bodies and take care of them if they're to last — which is why a lot of adults, even very rich ones, spend their time running on peculiar machines with rubber mats that go nowhere.

This is a book about your mind and how to keep it healthy by doing the equivalent of taking it to the gym. There are some basic ingredients you

will need for this kind of health. First of all, you will need to get a lot of sleep, as brains do all kinds of vital repair work while you're curled up in bed. It is also a good idea to eat the right sort of diet, as our brains work best when they've been fed healthy and delicious things like carrots and chickpea salads. But the most important thing your mind needs to keep it healthy is good ideas. This means ideas that can make you less worried, that can make life more interesting, that can calm you down when something has gone wrong, and that can stop you feeling too upset about situations you might be facing.

There are lots of problems we're already good at solving. If you're hungry, you can have a toasted sandwich. If you are cold, you can put on more clothes or turn up the heating. If you cut your finger you can put a plaster on it. If you have an ear infection, a doctor can give you some medicine. But there are other problems that are harder to deal with. Often these are mind problems. They are to do with your thoughts and feelings about something or someone that is upsetting you.

My dad keeps nagging me
My friend was mean to me
I'm actually very shy
I wish I was a bit more organised
My brother is so annoying
My mum yells at me
I am worried I am going to fail maths
I don't know what I want to be when I grow up
I said something mean to my friend

My classmates don't like the same things as me
I still can't spell well
Do my students think I'm boring?
I don't like my hair
Our teacher is boring
I wish I was taller
I wish my family would take me on a holiday
I cheated on my last test
My bedroom is very messy

Mind problems are normal. Everyone in your class has some, although they might have different ones from you. And all grown-ups have mind problems, although they might be about work or money or their families. Famous people have them too.

You probably don't know much about other people's mind problems. You don't know they've got them unless they tell you. Mostly we don't tell each other because no one wants to look strange, weak or in trouble (but all of us are like that sometimes, which means it is very normal to feel odd).

If you have a mind problem, putting a bandage around your head won't help. If you aren't having a good time at school, or if you feel shy or if you get upset with your parents, there isn't a pill you can take to make things better. But there *is* something that can help:

Learning new ideas

You already know quite a lot about learning new ideas and how helpful they can be.

Think about a 3-year-old who is building a tower with some bricks (they are very pleased that the tower is *four* bricks high). But another child is jumping around and bumps into them and knocks over the tower. The tower-building 3-year-old gets upset: 'I hate you, you broke my tower!' they might scream.

If you were trying to calm down that child, what might you say? Perhaps you would try to teach them about the idea of an 'accident'. A bad thing can happen, but the other person did not mean to do it. Realising that something can be an accident is an important and helpful idea. You had to learn it, and someone taught you — though you might not remember when. Now it is an idea you can bring out to calm someone down (in another situation, that person might be you).

Or imagine a 4-year-old who is worried that there might be a tiger hiding in a cupboard. What would you say to them? Maybe you'd just tell them not to be stupid. (Or maybe, if you were feeling mischievous, you'd scare them by telling them you'd seen the tiger and it looked very, very hungry.) But if you wanted to help them, you could ask them some questions in a friendly way, as if you were wondering too: where could the tiger have come from? If it came from the zoo, how could it have gone through the streets without anyone seeing it and telling the police? How could it get into the house? Wouldn't a tiger struggle to use a key with its claws? How could it open the cupboard door? How could it close the door from the inside? Would a tiger fit in the cupboard, given how much stuff is already in there?

You are asking questions but, really, what you are doing is giving the 4-year-old a big new *idea*: that you can look at a situation calmly and ask whether your fear could be real or not. A 4-year-old is only just beginning to realise that bad things can't just happen by a horrible kind of magic — or because they don't feel good inside. There has to be an explanation for how something difficult or dangerous can happen. Because you can't really explain how there could be a tiger in the cupboard, once you think about it, that's a strong sign that there isn't one. Thinking things through calmly helps — a lot. When you think about explanations, often your fears go away, because you realise that the thing you fear couldn't really happen. You learn a big lesson that many adults still try to keep in their minds: a fear is not a fact.

This is a book of ideas that can help you with mind problems. It is, if you like, the equivalent of going to a gym to keep your body healthy. But instead of lifting weights and pulling on ropes, we're going to be lifting up some ideas. Some will be quite heavy; some will be quite new. Others you'll have heard already from someone nice who loves you. But it's good to flex your brain anyway.

We're going to look at a range of mind problems you might encounter and talk about some of the best ideas your mind could use to deal with them. The result should be something very important: you'll have a healthier, happier mind and it will be more exciting to wake up to every new day.

Let's look at some mind problems and see what kinds of ideas might help with them.

CHAPTER 1

Parents

You didn't get to choose your parents

One of the weirdest things about being human is that our parents are a big deal. We are tiny and helpless for a long time. We need their help and support for twenty years at least, which is a pretty long period in which to be affected, for good and for bad, by their tastes and characters.

That is not the case with most other animals. A baby horse (a foal) is up and running about half an hour after it is born. It is pretty much fully grown before a human infant can say its first word. Many of the world's creatures don't even spend a minute with their parents: the average baby fish is left to its own devices the moment it emerges from its egg. The blue whale, which is the biggest living animal in the world, is fully developed by its fifth birthday.

But a typical human will spend 25,000 hours with its parents by the time they are 18. That's generally fantastic, because your parents love you more than pretty much anyone else, but it does bring complications too.

For many years, your parents are in charge of nearly everything about your life. They decide where you live and where you can go on holiday; they tell you what time you have to go to bed and what food you should eat. They decide what to buy and what's too expensive. You often need them to take you places and when their friends come around, you have no option but to say hello to them.

There are other important ways in which your parents might influence you. If you have a dad who is interested in cooking, you might know a lot of different dishes; maybe he talks a lot about the right setting for the oven or he's shown you how to use a rolling pin. Or, if your mum is really interested in music, maybe you've heard a lot of songs other people at school don't know about. Maybe a parent coached you at tennis or was keen on you playing the trombone or wants you to read a lot.

Perhaps your parents are always watching the news or maybe they never watch it. Is your house very tidy or pretty messy? That depends on the adults. When you picture your family having a meal, do you see yourself sitting around the table with lots of people telling interesting stories, or sitting on the sofa while you watch a film together? Both might be nice, but they are very different. If there's a problem, do the adults react calmly or do they get in a panic? Are they always late or are they focused on being on time?

You don't think about all this when you are a baby, but as you grow, you become aware of a new big idea:

Your parents
are people too

And they can be quite a bit different from other people's parents. What your grown-ups are like makes a huge difference to your life. If you had other parents, your routines would be completely different: maybe you wouldn't even be very much like you (which is a puzzling idea).

Even though your parents are probably the most important people in your life, crucially, you didn't get to choose them. There are usually some big gaps between what you could imagine a parent being like and how an actual parent really is...

But hold on! Here's another strange thought: *your parents did not know what you would be like.*

Will they like magic tricks?

What will they be like when they are 11? Or 18? Or 45?

Maybe they'll be cleverer than me

I wonder if they'll like to go swimming with me?

Will they laugh at my jokes?

I hope they are happy

Small children think their parents know everything and can do anything. But as you get a bit older you start to realise they can get things wrong. Maybe they can't dance or they don't know how to spell a word. Maybe they sleep too much or complain about work, or they try to tell a joke but it's not funny. You discover there are ways parents can be *annoying*.

Ways parents are annoying

PARENTS CAN BE FUSSY

They tell you that you need a hat or a coat, even though you do not feel cold; they want to make you eat broccoli because they claim it will help you live longer. If you want to climb a rock they'll tell you it's dangerous; they constantly ask you if you have brushed your teeth properly.

You know it's annoying but, to calm your mind down, there's a question you should ask: *why* do they fuss? What's going on in their brains? It's not really because they are horrible. There are other explanations.

Parents fuss because, for a long time, they had to. When you were a baby, you were fragile and they had to worry a lot. If you got cold you might start to cry, or get sick. If you went near some stairs you'd probably fall down them. If you didn't eat the right things you'd not grow properly. When you were very small, you didn't realise a car might bump into you, so your parents had to be careful every time you went outside. You couldn't brush your own teeth, so they had to do it for you. You can't remember much of it, but it went on for years. So a parent's brain gets into the habit of always worrying about what might go wrong, and it's hard for them to switch off this habit, even when you get older and they don't need to worry so much.

Here's a useful definition of a parent: a person who will always believe that their child is a baby, and needs as much looking after as a baby did, even when they're 20 or 53. That's just a fact — and if you look at how your grandparents treat your mum and dad, you'll probably see evidence. For your granny, your dad is still 2 years old!

We're not saying that this is sensible; it just seems to be the way it is. It's best to accept it, as you would a rainy day.

But let's focus on something else. Remember that people usually get bothered most about things that they care a lot about. If you are really interested in flags, it would bother you if someone mixed up the flag of France and the flag of Russia.

They'd say *you* were being fussy. But you'd say you were *really interested*.

There's no one in the world your parents are more interested in than you. They probably don't fuss so much around anything or anyone else. It *is* annoying, but your parents probably are not fussy around people in general (they've probably never tried to brush their friends' hair or asked their colleagues if they were eating enough vegetables).

They are fussy about you, and their fussing basically means: 'I love you.' The big idea here is:

Parents are fussy
because they love you

This is important: it's an idea to help you when things are difficult around your parents. Understanding *why* a parent fusses doesn't stop them from doing it. It doesn't make the fussing seem any more sensible or right (it really can't matter that much whether you have a carrot every day or not). What it changes is your idea of what they are doing when they bother you with their fussing. They're *trying* to help you have the best life they think you can have, even though the way they're doing it is annoying and might even be rather wrong. They're *trying* to be nice, even though it's not nice for you.

Now, change tack a bit and think about *why* fussing annoys you. It *is* upsetting, but there's a big, new question to ask: *why* is it so upsetting? Is it more upsetting now than ever? Maybe what is bothering you is that they are fussing *because they still think I'm a baby. They have not noticed I'm older.* And this is a new and increasingly big worry for you.

Let's face it. It's nice to grow up. It is exciting when you're older and you can do so many more things than in the past. You get better at playing football; you can read better; you can go to a more interesting party; you can ride a bike properly. When you are 8, it seems silly to be 6. When you are 10, it feels silly to be 8.

When a parent fusses, it's as if they are saying that you are only 6 (when you are actually 8) or that you are 8 (when you are actually 10). Haven't they noticed that you can do things for yourself? Don't they understand that lots of things are now up to you? They seem to be sending you backwards.

But there's more to think about. You can still ask: why is *that* a problem? What is it about some annoying things that means we get upset, while with others we stay fairly calm?

Imagine you are good at running. You win lots of races, and you know you can run faster than anyone else in your class. Someone comes up to you and says: 'You are terrible at running'. Does that upset you? Probably not. You probably don't care, because you are sure in your own mind about what you can do. They are wrong and it doesn't matter what they say.

So here's a new thought: we get upset when people pick up on our own doubts about ourselves. (It's not just you: grown-ups do this all the time as well.) But if we can feel sure about ourselves, other people's reactions don't bother us so much.

In terms of you and your parents, what this means is: you don't need to get your parents to stop fussing (which is good news, because you probably can't stop them). What you can do is change how you think and feel about what they are doing when they fuss. More specifically, you need to be sure of an odd-sounding but crucial idea:

You aren't going to go
back to being a baby

You were small then, but you're much bigger now. And you're never going backwards. The more you know this deep in yourself, the less their fussing will annoy you. You know that you can look after your own hair, and you can have your own ideas about how tidy your room should be. You know whether you are cold or not. You know you have your own thoughts about the world and your place in it. A fussy parent might not know everything about you, but you do. And if you are sure, it matters less what they think. It's still a *bit* annoying but, armed with a sure sense of yourself, not as much as it was.

This is a general and big idea to help your mind: the more you know your truth — the truth about you — the less other people's difficult or wrong ideas will matter, and the less you'll be bothered if someone else believes something about you that you feel isn't true. Changing people's minds is always harder than working on our own minds, so concentrate on getting sure about who you are. It will make the wrong-headed ideas of others matter much less. They will wash over us like rain on a car windscreen.

There are two ways to get peace of mind: ensure that no one ever says anything untrue about you, or work on feeling very sure deep in yourself about the things you know are true.

The second option is the easiest — and the wisest!

PARENTS ARE EMBARRASSING

You worry that other people, and especially people at school, will think your parents are strange. Maybe your mum has funny hair or your dad wears unusual clothes. Perhaps one of them has a foreign accent or a big red face — it could be a million things. For a long time it didn't bother you; they were just your parents, and that was that. But now, increasingly, you worry about what other people think. You worry your friends might make jokes about your parents — and that they might say you are odd too, because you are the offspring of parents who wear green glasses or swear a lot while hanging pictures. If someone says something mean (but that is sort of true), you blush and feel awkward; you might feel like crying.

I wish my parents were normal...

Little children will never get embarrassed because their brains have not developed enough to imagine what other people might be thinking. They are too focused on their own thoughts and priorities (like stacking things up or seeing what it is like to put spaghetti on their head, or pulling a teddy bear's ears off). That you're starting to wonder what your friend at school thinks about your parents is a sign that your mind has grown pretty complicated. That normally means two things: you've got new powers, and you've got new possibilities for feeling unhappy.

One big reason you think that your parents are odd is that you know a lot more about them than you do about other people's parents. You see them when they are upset or in a panic. You see them early in the morning with their hair all messed up. You hear them complaining about silly things or shouting at the television, or singing loudly in the shower. You know what they said when they spilt tomato sauce all over their trousers. But you don't have these experiences around other people's parents, though there are probably ways in which they are just as mad and silly.

The same thing happens to other children. They know all the odd things about *their* parents; they think *their* parents are embarrassing and that *yours* are normal.

The stories we tell ourselves — at school or in the newspaper or on TV — about what is normal don't reflect what really is normal. We go around pretending that no one has strange thoughts or that no one's parents are eccentric or that no one sometimes wants a cuddle as if they were still 4 years old.

That's why it can be helpful to keep a big and kind idea in mind:

No one is normal

That doesn't mean everyone is wacky: they aren't. It's just that real life can be a lot weirder than we tend to admit. And that's OK. Every family is a bit unusual; every mum or dad has their distinctive habits. If you put a TV camera into anyone's house and watched what was going on, there would be some surprising stuff — stuff that people would call 'weird' but that was just part of what human beings are like.

The thing that helps when people try to embarrass you is *imagination*. Your mind can make pictures of things you haven't seen. You can imagine what other people's lives might really be like even when they aren't telling you. They might seem strong and confident, but you can imagine them getting angry or feeling worried. They might seem sure of themselves, but you can imagine them realising they've made a big mistake or shutting their finger in the door by accident. If you're scared of someone, imagine they've just discovered, too late, that they've run out of toilet paper, or imagine them picking their nose when they think no one is looking. The next time someone tells you that your family is odd and suggests theirs is not, imagine the many ways in which their situation might be distinctive in its own way.

Or you could simply get this T-shirt made up for you to wear, which makes the point even better:

Your parents may love you very much, but that doesn't mean they always listen to you as well as they might. That's not a special failing of theirs. Human beings may have pretty good ears, but they don't tend to use them as often as they should.

One of our deepest hopes is that other people will listen to our feelings properly. We don't want others necessarily to agree with all our feelings, but what we crave is that they at least hear them. Often they don't. Here are some examples of how parents don't really listen.

I'm feeling a bit sad

Don't be silly, you can't be sad; it's the holidays

I am really worried

That's ridiculous, there's nothing to be scared of

I wish there wasn't any school ever again

Come on! You know we have to leave the house by eight

In a perfect world — a world in which parents did always listen — it would be different. For example, the conversation could be:

I'm feeling a bit sad

Weird, isn't it, how you can be sad at the oddest of times, even at the beach

I am really worried

I can see why you're scared: the wind is fierce out here

I wish there wasn't any school ever again

It must be horrible having maths all morning, especially after such a nice weekend

But let's use our imagination machines again and ask: *why* don't parents listen well all the time?

One explanation (for this and for lots of other parent problems) is: our parents are *evil*.

But that is unlikely to be the case. There might be a few genuinely evil parents around, but there's a far more likely explanation: they're scared and they're worried.

This is a good general rule: whenever people seem evil, ask yourself a big question. Might this person be scared and worried instead? What might they be scared of or worried about? If you keep that thought in mind, it changes your life.

What is it parents might be afraid of when they don't listen to you? Here is an idea: they care so much about you, they don't want to imagine that you are suffering, and so they shut their ears to inconvenient things you are saying; for example, that you're sad or don't like school.

Also, because your parents worry a lot about your future (they shouldn't, but they feel responsible), they tend to shut their ears to information that suggests your future might be difficult. They worry that you might turn into someone who isn't polite or who never gets a job, so they find it hard to hear when you say you hate their friends or don't want to do your homework. It isn't that they don't care, it's just that they're panicking.

What parents forget is that your feelings, especially difficult feelings, are going to get better once they've been listened to properly. If your parents listen more carefully when you say how much you hate your teachers, you might not want to be cheeky at school any more. If you were allowed to moan a bit more about going to Granny's house, you mightn't mind going so much. Feelings get less strong, not more strong, as soon as they have been given an airing. We moan when no one's listened, never because they listened too much. What you might ask your parent to do, instead, when you have something to tell them, is just to say, 'Wow, tell me more…'

You can remember that, if you become a parent. By the way, at difficult moments in your childhood, there's something very nice that you can do in your mind. You can open a file in your mind-computer called *What I'll Never Do With My Own Children*. Add in big and small ideas as they occur to you. You'll soon have quite a long list. When you're older, open up the file and see what's in it. Some ideas will still seem sensible, and you'll have a thrilling feeling that you're doing things better than your parents.

Others might not look so good, and then you will be able to call up your parents and laugh about stuff. Either way, you'll win.

The good news about the not-listening problem is that it's easy to fix. You can fix it with your friends and you can even help your parents to fix it. All you need to do is play someone's feelings back to them, as if you were a kind of tape recorder or a mirror. When someone says, 'I am upset...' rather than change the subject or say 'No, you're not,' you can say, 'Oh wow, tell me more...' Or when they say: 'That makes me so angry', rather than say, 'It's bad to be angry', say: 'I can see you must be frustrated...' (that calms people down very fast! Try it!).

Crucially, we don't need to be listened to by everyone. We can bear an awful lot of feelings when just a few people listen to us. You can try to grow into one of those valuable people who listen a lot.

PARENTS ARE HYPOCRITES

A hypocrite is someone who tells you not to do something *and then goes off and does it themselves.*

Grown-ups quite often look like hypocrites. They say you shouldn't check your phone so much, *then they check theirs!* They tell you not to eat so much chocolate, then you discover they have a secret stash at the back of a cupboard. They tell you you should read more books, but they don't read any books. They tell you to be kind but then they say mean things about other people. There's a gap between what your parents *tell you to do* and *what they do.*

Why don't parents live by their own rules? Why do they do what they tell you not to do? There's quite a good answer to this, but it can sound a bit strange at first. Very often, a parent doesn't like what they do. They wish they didn't eat so much chocolate; they wish they didn't watch so much TV. They still do these things, but they'd rather not do them. They don't know how to stop themselves doing them, so they want to stop you — not to lie to you or hurt you, but because:

Parents want you to have
a better life than they had

This sounds peculiar because, when we're very little, we think that our parents are in charge of everything. They can do what they want, and they only do things because they want to. But as we grow up, we start to see something odd: grown-ups aren't in control of their lives or of themselves as much as we think. They get things wrong. They have feelings they wish they didn't. They don't have complete command over themselves. They have thoughts they can't get rid of. They act younger than their age. They might be 45 and, maybe when they're tired, act like someone who's 9. That's strange, but it happens to everyone! Despite all this, they want to help you avoid the mistakes they make.

Imagine you don't like doing homework. You put it off as long as you can, and you find it really difficult to make an effort. Maybe you *wish* you could do it easily and quickly, but you struggle with it. Now think about far into the future: imagine *you* are a parent. You might try hard to get your child to do *their* homework, and they might say, 'You're a hypocrite: you told me you didn't do your homework when you were my age.' Is that fair? Maybe not. But it would be a sign of kindness. You just wouldn't want them to struggle the way you struggled.

A parent doesn't usually want you to turn into them. They hope you'll end up being better than them. A parent who eats too many biscuits hopes you'll snack on apples; a parent who is a bit lazy hopes you will be bursting with energy; if they worry they're wasting their time watching too much TV, they hope you'll have more interesting hobbies. So maybe it's a bit unfair to call a parent a hypocrite: they're something more interesting. They are people with regrets about themselves, and hopes — and a deep love — for you.

PARENTS ARGUE ABOUT STUPID THINGS

Parents choose to be together; they could each have chosen to be with someone else. But they did not. They chose each other. So you'd think they'd be happy with one another. But often they get grumpy and quarrel. And often it's about things that don't seem to matter at all.

Maybe one of them gets cross because the curtains aren't closed the right way or because the tomatoes are in the wrong part of the fridge. Perhaps they argue about whether a suitcase is packed properly or about what time they need to leave to get to the airport. Maybe one of them gets worked up about what's on the news and the other doesn't and they argue about that. Or they argue about whether to go to a party or whether they need to get a new hairdryer or whether the house is tidy or messy. For most parents it's a long list. Even if they don't always argue out loud, you can feel they are getting upset and annoyed and that's just as bad.

Why do they argue? They argue because they are tired, often. And because they too want life to look the way they picture it inside their heads and get cross when it doesn't. And because they care, and want the person they spend most time with to care about the things they care about.

But some of the things they care about seem so stupid! You don't care about any of these things, so why should they get so worked up about them? Why are your parents so idiotic about the way they argue?

There's quite a clever way you can understand what's happening. Think about your own life and the things that matter to you now and compare them with things that used to matter to you. Maybe you can't remember what you cared about, so we've suggested some possibilities:

WHEN YOU WERE 2

Having a parent around all the time; splashing in the bath; my knitted rabbit; putting on my jumper all by myself!

3 YEARS AGO

Trains; flags; drawing a windmill; my pop-up book; pretending to be a puppy; my new blue shorts

NOW

What my friend said about me; long division; YouTube; sailing; shoes; prank videos; games; the shape of my nose

Can you spot something? Can you see how the things you care about have changed? They have been changing quite fast over the last few years.

You can understand how you would get upset if someone you were with a lot of the time didn't agree with you about some of the things that mean a lot to you. A 2-year-old would be devastated if someone did not like their plastic frog or knitted rabbit. If you like a particular YouTube channel, you'd get upset if someone said it was stupid. But to a 2-year-old it would seem silly to get worked up about that. That's because a 2-year-old can't see why you care. But you do, and in time they will probably understand.

There's an odd thought about growing up. The more you grow up, the more you will care about things. If you were colouring in a map to show 'the things I care about', the coloured area would grow larger and larger with time. By the time you're an adult, you might care about the shape of the light switch in the hall and whether a book should be arranged vertically or horizontally.

Imagine extending these thoughts into the future. What things might you care about in a few years' time or when you are the same age as your parents? It's a tricky question. Have a go and write down your ideas (you can look back in 2075 and see if you were right). We have made some suggestions to get you started.

The point is, when you are older you will care about lots of things that seem strange or ridiculous now. They aren't. It's just that the empire of what we care about keeps spreading — and we want our friends, or our partner, to share as many of our tastes as possible.

When I'm 17...

SUGGESTIONS

What should I study? How do you get a job? Should I get my driver's license? What are my friends doing today?

YOUR IDEAS

When I'm 26...

SUGGESTIONS

Why are my friends earning more money than me? How do you buy a house? Who will I marry? Should I move?

YOUR IDEAS

When I'm 40...

SUGGESTIONS

Should I start a business? What happens if they call an election? Where can I buy nice napkins for a dinner party?

YOUR IDEAS

When I'm 65...

SUGGESTIONS

Where do I invest my money? What do I get my son-in-law for Christmas? Should I paint the bathroom duck-egg blue?

YOUR IDEAS

Although most parents squabble and get cross with each other from time to time, sometimes it is more serious. Maybe they do not want to stay together any more — or at least one of them doesn't. Perhaps they have separated already.

It can feel very sad. But here's a big reason why it can feel even sadder than it should. At some level, you may suspect that you have done something wrong. Maybe you feel as if your parents aren't getting on or are unhappy or are breaking up because of the way you are: you're to blame. It sounds too awful to think about.

In Papua New Guinea, there's a tribe called the Huli who live in the middle mountainous part of the country. In the middle of the 20th century, some Australian professors went to study them. They recorded their language and took careful note of their ways of cooking and hunting. One thing that struck the Australians was that whenever there was a dramatic thunderstorm, the Huli would explain it like this: they believed that someone in the tribe had done something bad and that the weather was a punishment for this badness from an angry spirit. The Australians had grown up to believe that thunderstorms were the result of warm air colliding with cool air (maybe you've learnt about that in geography), and they couldn't imagine that it had anything to do with angry spirits. But to the Huli, it seemed natural to suppose that if the sky was looking angry, it had to be angry *with them*, probably about some bad thing they'd done and not told anyone else about (we all have those things).

We might know that the Huli are not right, but the way they think tells us something interesting about how all our minds work. It is easy to imagine that when bad, dramatic, loud or scary things unfold around us, it's because we're somehow to blame. All of us are inclined to think this way. We think: 'Maybe I've done something wrong... and that's why the sky is full of lightning'; or 'that's why I'm getting sick', or 'that's why Mum and Dad are shouting...'

Because it can be easy to think this way, and because it really doesn't help, here's a big thought you might write up somewhere prominent, on a big piece of paper or on a T-shirt.

Without knowing your parents or you, we can still be sure of one thing. Your parents aren't arguing or breaking up because of you. Their break-up will affect you, but it isn't caused by you. We can promise you that.

The business of living together is complicated. You know that because you probably squabble with a sibling — or at least know people who do. You can't divorce a sibling, but if people could, there'd be a lot of divorced brothers and sisters wandering the world.

It's no different with adults. Remember that if you have a very good friend, you probably only see them some of the time. But imagine if you went on holiday with them and suppose the holiday didn't just last for a week, or two weeks, but for two years, or ten years. After a while, tiny things about them would start to bother you. Maybe you wouldn't completely agree on who was in charge when you played a game. After a month you might get fed up with this tension; after a year you might be desperate. Or maybe your friend is a bit bossy; it doesn't matter too much, because they're fun in lots of other ways and your play dates tend to last only an afternoon. But if you were with them for a decade, you might now be quite unhappy.

This is what sometimes happens with grown-ups. They really like each other, but when they try to live together all the time, problems start to emerge. They do not like the same things; they want to go on different kinds of holidays; they find different things funny; they have diverging views of what a nice evening might involve, or even how to bring you up.

Gradually, it becomes difficult for them to eat a meal together without getting cross. They've done well in a way; they may have been together for ten years or more, but they can't imagine doing it for another ten years. Remember, too, that grown-ups aren't excellent in all subjects. They can be good at one thing and not very good at something else — like you can be good at maths but not good at running; or good at looking after pets but quite bad at keeping your bedroom tidy.

Many grown-ups aren't very good at a topic called 'Living with someone else', but that doesn't mean they can't be nice, kind or intelligent — and, especially, good at looking after and loving you.

Being together and looking after a child are two very different projects. Generally, loving a child comes a lot more naturally to most adults than loving another adult. It has to do with expectations. Adults expect an awful lot from their partners. They want them to understand them, to cheer them up, to be their best friend all the time, to be on their side, to be interesting as well as helpful, to be punctual and good at cooking.

Yet parents tend not to expect nearly as much from their children, thank goodness. They may be grateful if you give them a kiss every now and then, and try to make conversation over supper, but they didn't put you on this earth in order for you to answer all their needs. They understood that a child can't listen to all their problems, soothe them when they're anxious or cheer them up when they're down.

Yet when it comes to their adult partners, they do have many such hopes and more — which is what can make them intolerant and quick to lose their tempers. That points us to another big idea for life:

The more you expect of people...

...the more angry you'll be when people aren't perfect

Sometimes, one of the nicest things you can do with someone you care for is not to expect too much from them. Maybe you can love them and accept that they'll always have lots of things about them that aren't ideal. To think someone is completely great sounds flattering, but it's a recipe for trouble. If we were redesigning how people get married, we'd want to advise people to head into weddings with different expectations.

To repeat, the fact that your parents don't get on together doesn't mean they don't care about you. They might exchange angry words with one another, but they continue to love you as they've always done, from the moment you were born, as they'll probably have told you lots of times already. You should believe them.

Understanding your parents

When you are very little, you never think you might need to understand your parents. Later you might start to feel that your parents don't properly understand you. But there's another project you might get interested in: the project of becoming curious about who your parents really are. This can be fun.

Part of the problem is that your parents have always been around, so you don't get curious about them as you might a stranger. But imagine you were meeting them for the first time. What would you want to know?

It can be interesting to look at old photos of your parents. If there is a picture of your mum on the beach aged 9 and a half, what was happening? Was she on holiday? Did she like swimming? Or maybe there's a picture of your dad wearing a school uniform or playing chess or sitting on a new

bike. Would you have been friends with him, if you had been around then? Your parents have probably had a lot more experiences like yours than you suppose, only you haven't heard about them yet. You could ask them questions when everyone is relaxed. Here are some questions you might ask your parents:

What were they like when they were 7 years old? Or 10? Or when they were 13?

What was fun for them? What did they worry about? Did they ever feel lonely?

What was their day like? What did they like to eat? Did they watch TV?

What was their house like? Can they describe their room? What did they do after school?

How did they get to school? Who was their favourite teacher? What did they do at lunchtime?

Did they get on with their parents? Did they argue much? Were they strict? Did they ever feel embarrassed by them?

How did they imagine themselves in the future?

There's a funny thing about asking questions. Often we ask about facts: where were they, what happened, who was there? But really we're trying to imagine *what it was like being them*. How did they feel? Were they happy or sad? Were they confident or nervous? What funny thoughts were going on inside their head that they didn't tell people about?

If you understand your parents better, you'll probably end up feeling that they understand you better.

A report card for parents

There are lots of things people don't know how to do, unless someone teaches them: drive a bus, fly a jet plane or perform surgery to correct someone's eyesight. If you tried to do these things without having lots of lessons and guidance and training it would be a disaster. You wouldn't even try because you know these are skills that take a long time to learn. If someone doesn't have a skill, we don't blame them, though we might try to teach them.

When you think about it, being a parent involves lots of skills, but no one really teaches parents how to be parents. Here are some of the tricky things parents try to do.

WORK OUT WHAT YOU THINK AND FEEL

Sometimes you get upset or excited, but it's not easy to put into words what's bothering you or why something is so nice. A parent can see that *something* is on your mind, but they don't automatically know what it is.

It's a special skill to ask questions, make suggestions, look carefully for clues, be patient and imaginative.

TAKE AN INTEREST IN WHAT YOU'VE BEEN DOING WITHOUT BEING NOSY

It's quite a delicate balance. If a parent asks 'What have you been up to?' it can feel as if they are trying to spy on you. If they don't ask, it feels as if they don't care.

It's odd to think that some people have jobs as interviewers, because it means they're amazingly good at getting other people to tell them things — but most of us are not so good at this. No one gets lessons in how to ask good questions and how to listen. We're expected just to know how to do these things, but it is a difficult and important skill.

CALM YOU DOWN WHEN YOU ARE UPSET

Part of a parent's job is to make you feel less worried or bothered when you are upset. But it's not an easy job. How do you do that? How do you reassure someone, without pretending that their problem isn't real? How do you take someone's mind off something that's upsetting them? And how do you do it when maybe no one ever showed you?

GETTING YOU TO DO SOMETHING WITHOUT BEING TOO BOSSY

Every day, there are lots of things you have to do that maybe you don't want to do. A parent has to make sure you get to school on time, that you've brushed your teeth, that you eat healthy food, that you don't go to bed too late.

It is difficult to get anyone to do things they do not want to do without being bossy. But if you are bossy, people start to get annoyed. So there's a delicate art of persuading without irritating. It's possible to learn how to do this, but hardly anyone gets taught properly.

EXPLAIN THINGS IN WAYS THAT HELP YOU UNDERSTAND

There are lots of things you know how to do, but it's not easy to explain them to anyone else. Imagine that you had to explain how to speak your language to someone who didn't know it: it would be incredibly difficult. Suppose you had to explain how to ride a bike or tie a pair of shoe laces.

Explaining isn't easy. Parents have to explain things all the time: why is school important; what is politics about; why you need to visit Granddad at the weekend, even if you'd rather stay at home — and lots and lots of other things.

But there is a small problem:

Parents don't get lessons
in 'how to explain things'

At school you might get a report on how you are doing in various subjects. It's a statement about how your skills are developing in different ways. Parents are trying to develop skills too, so you could give them a report.

For each of the skills we've been describing, give a parent a grade:

A

DISTINCTION

They're really great
at doing this

B

COMMENDATION

Not always great
but fairly good

C

PASS

They do try but the
results are poor

D

MUST IMPROVE

Not very good; how
can they improve?

Think about what grades you would give your parents for each of the five skills on the next page and write them in the medals on their report card.

Usually we think of report cards as messages to students. But they are also messages to the teacher. If a child isn't doing well in some areas, that teacher can think about how they can help. Is there something they need to do? How could they help the student improve? If you are giving a report on a parent, you are like the teacher. How could you help your parents get better around the things they are not getting right? Maybe you could help them develop their skills.

SKILL 1

Helps you work out how you feel, even
when you don't quite know yourself

SKILL 2

Gets you to chat about what you're
doing without being a bit too nosy

SKILL 3

Can calm you down when you're feeling
upset, annoyed, angry or distressed

SKILL 4

Gets you to do things that you need
to do without being too bossy

SKILL 5

Explains all sorts of things in ways
that help you understand

CHAPTER 2

Screens

Why screens are so nice

There are times when it feels as if all you want to do is keep looking at a screen, watching a video or playing a game. Pretty much nothing else is as nice. You might be on holiday in a beautiful place or it might be your uncle's birthday. But frankly, that doesn't seem to matter. What you really want to do is keep scrolling through posts, play games and watch prank videos on YouTube.

This makes your parents furious, although they might use their screens a lot too. There are few subjects on which adults and children argue more about than screens. Perhaps your father once suggested, and it almost felt as if he meant it, that he'd take your machine and put a large nail right through the middle of it. How silly!

But have you ever thought about *why* screens have such a strong grip of our attention? It's not because anyone is bad or weak-willed.

The answer is pretty strange: *it's to do with how our brains evolved.*

To see how this works, let's start by thinking about some other things we tend to really like and can't stop turning to, even if they're not healthy for us: cakes, chocolate, biscuits and ice cream.

For almost the whole time that humans have existed, for hundreds of thousands of years, there were very few sweet things to eat — only apples, or bananas, or the odd strawberry, and then only for a short time of the year — and all sweet things were good for us. So our brains evolved to get excited by anything sweet, because it was a sign of something extremely important to our diet.

Then, around the middle of the 20th century, it became cheap to make sweet things, and the problems began. Our brains kept wanting more and more junk food and they couldn't tell the difference between a cola and a mango. Our brains remained the same, but as the environment changed, some of our tastes grew harmful to us. It's now rare to find a middle-aged adult — probably your mum or dad — who doesn't worry about their weight.

Something similar has happened around things we can watch. Imagine that you were living a long, long time ago. There was no TV, there was hardly any entertainment, and there was nothing like a computer. Our brains developed a habit of paying special attention to all small, quick movements, to any news from somewhere else and to anything bright and shiny. All these once signalled important things: perhaps a snake (if you lived somewhere hot), or maybe a wasp (if it was summer); or maybe vital news from another tribe or village.

Our brains became engineered to be very interested in things to hunt, in colourful movements, and in information about other people; this made perfect sense 10,000 years ago.

Today, our brains still work in the same way: their deep habits haven't changed. But now all the content on our screens that activates them is not connected to any real danger or advantage. Our brains keep on getting excited even though the original good reasons for that excitement are not involved. Our screens trick our brains into thinking: 'This is really important,' just as the deluxe chocolate bar can trick our stomachs into thinking: 'You have to eat this now...' The big idea here is that:

Sometimes our brain tricks us into thinking something bad is good for us

It's not our fault that our brains are like this, but it causes us problems that we should become curious about.

Probably your parents have said to you, 'You're addicted to that machine.' The normal response is to ask them to be quiet, or to laugh them off. But what does this accusation of *addiction* really mean?

Am I an addict?

The concept of addiction is a bit odd. Probably you've seen a homeless person nursing a bottle of wine or beer and your parents have said, 'That's an addict.' An addict appears to be someone who finds drinks so tasty, they just can't help but spend all their money on them, even if it means going without a comfortable home or shoes. It's a hard idea to get your head around, especially when wine or beer tastes so strange (you could just about imagine becoming a Coca-Cola addict... but not really!).

However, it's time to stretch our ideas of what addiction means. Addiction is a pattern of behaviour in which you get really drawn to one exciting thing because you are trying to escape from doing or feeling something else that's somehow difficult (even if it may be worthwhile).

What properly indicates addiction is not *what* someone is addicted to, because we can get addicted to pretty much anything. It is *why*: an addict is someone who is using something as a way to avoid looking at something else in their lives that's making them anxious or daunted.

So we might be addicted to the news because we really don't want to call Granny and listen to her sad stories about her hip operation. Or we might be addicted to exercise because it stops us having to feel worried about our work that's not going so well. Or we might be addicted to going out because it stops us being alone and having to face up to confused feelings about a friend who is being mean to us.

Your mother might get addicted to a TV show when she's avoiding feeling sadness about her brother. Your father might feel addicted to his phone because there's a project he needs to do, but really doesn't want to start.

We shouldn't call ourselves non-addicts just because we aren't drinking vodka all day. You could be an addict and people might not even notice. Nowadays, the most respectable kind of addiction is screen addiction — and what makes you an addict isn't just being on your screen all the time, it is the fact that you are running to a screen because you're running away from something else.

Maybe you would like to spend less time on the screen. But the way to do this isn't just to be angry at yourself. You shouldn't feel ashamed of your strong impulse to go on the screen; that never works. The trick is to ask yourself what you're scared of, what you're worried about doing or what you're trying to avoid. You need to feel safe about confronting your need to do something else that's a bit difficult, but probably a lot more valuable: like starting some homework, or having a tricky conversation with a friend, or realising that your beloved grandfather is getting really old and you may miss him a lot when he isn't there any more.

So, next time someone calls you a 'screen addict', try thinking of yourself as someone who is really worried or really uncomfortable about doing something else — and not because you are lazy but because it is really hard. Even better, tell someone who loves you about your fears, anxieties and reluctance. Rather than letting them label you, reveal what's on your mind, what's really worrying you, what you're scared of. Ask them to help you with everything that's much more difficult than looking at a screen.

It's a lot more charming and effective to say: 'Maybe I am a bit of a screen addict! Now help me...' You could try it next time that argument comes around again, as it will.

Words without people

One odd thing about technology is that you see words without seeing the person who is writing them. Think about this book. You can see the words, but you can't see the team of people who put them together. That's even more true of screens, when you see words that someone's written on a blog or on your social media page.

This can be a problem because we can get unfairly scared or intimidated by words without people. Our brains evolved for a different situation: that of judging people and their words together, using the information from their face, their clothes and their manner to help us make sense of what they were saying.

Imagine if, way back in our prehistoric past, someone had said 'You did something wrong'. How would you react? It would depend on who was saying it. Suppose it was the person in charge of your tribe, someone that all the grown-ups listened to and who was really good at finding things for you all to eat. You'd take what they had to say seriously. But suppose it was a child from the next tent. You'd know they were pretty silly; you'd have spotted that they were in trouble this morning, maybe their face was muddy, or maybe they'd just been crying. You probably wouldn't worry about what they said; you might even feel sorry for them.

For thousands of years, you could decide if what someone said mattered or not as you were able to see them, and could bring your knowledge of who they were to your judgement of their words.

What happens today is that when we see words, or perhaps an image someone has posted, we forget to think properly about who has put them there. If someone sends a nasty message, we imagine that they must be intelligent and wise, happy and confident, and that their words come from a place of great knowledge and insight into us. We imagine that they must be essentially right in their views of us (even if what they're telling us is that we don't deserve to exist — which no one on the planet should ever tell anyone else). That's what makes us feel much worse about the words we read online and can lead us to feel anxious when we look at social media.

We have to remember that we don't know much about the people who leave nasty messages. If we saw them in real life, we might think them ridiculous and immediately understand that they weren't worth listening to. We'd recognise their desperate eyes and untrustworthy mouth and we'd dismiss most of what they were saying.

Nowadays, we can't know all the people who leave the messages that we see online, and that's why we can get so upset by the nastiness. But we do know something: they're just another human being. This isn't God speaking; it's a person. And we know something else, an important idea:

Kind people are the only
people you should respect

There's no excuse for bullying. So the moment you see something bad online, ignore it. There is no good reason ever to say nasty things online. If you come across such words, simply disregard them.

We can spare a thought for the horrible people who leave bad stuff online. No one wants to be brutal or cruel. They are that way because they are hurt, damaged, alone and afraid — and because no one has been kind or good to them for a long time. Behind every online outburst, there's always a sad backstory (we will mostly never know it, but we can be sure there is one) that has made it impossible for the commenter to feel they can be reasonable or nice. People get rude too, because — isolated behind a screen — it is impossible for them to believe that others out there could be hurt by their insults. They forget the power their words might have.

After spending a while online, it can be very easy to form the belief that humans have grown into monsters. The good news is that even though online stuff does reflect how the world is, it represents the fringe views of only a tiny percentage. They speak up instead of the majority of moderate, reasonable, kind, not terribly opinionated individuals who stand by in silence. The world is much saner than it appears. The real achievement would be to build an online world every bit as kind, patient and good as most of us are in our real lives at every moment of every day. Until then, ignore the nastiness you see online. It's the work of people you wouldn't give any time to if they were forced to emerge from behind their words.

Other people's perfect lives

There is another problem with the online world: the misery that is created by believing too much in the pictures people post of their lives — lives that seem very different from, and much nicer than, our own lives.

To get a handle on the problem, we should probably go to a museum and look at some pictures of people in times very remote from our own.

In London, at the National Gallery, there is a large room with pictures painted in the 18th century. Quite a few of them were by a clever artist, Thomas Gainsborough, who grew very famous by painting members of the English aristocracy. Like this painting of a couple called Mr and Mrs William Hallett on a walk with their dog.

Thomas Gainsborough, *Mr and Mrs William Hallett ('The Morning Walk')*, 1785

Many of Gainsborough's pictures are quite similar: the people in them are beautiful and calm. The weather is always good; there are always leaves on the trees; everyone looks well fed, clean, happy and respectable. The men wear stockings, the women beautifully embroidered dresses. And no one ever has egg stains on their trousers or lettuce in their teeth.

Because Gainsborough was so successful, it can be easy to think that the whole of 18th-century England looked like his paintings. But that is to forget about all the sides of that time that would have been very different and did not feature in the artwork. Gainsborough didn't paint anyone poor, sad or in a bad mood. That is not to say that kind of stuff didn't go on in 18th-century England. Of course it did, and a lot worse too. It's just that the pictures we're seeing are carefully chosen moments from a way of life that — then as now — also included arguments and temper tantrums, tears and shouting, despair and rage.

All this is a way of saying that when you go to an online 'gallery' and see pictures of smiling people looking beautiful by palm trees, remember that — just like Gainsborough — these are carefully selected moments. This isn't the whole of anyone's life. Away from the camera, those perfect people might wonder if they're any good, might be cross with their friends or uncertain about the future. Right next to the palm tree, just out of view, there might be an ugly hotel or unfinished motorway. We're being given a small glimpse into lives that are, in reality, rather different and always much more complicated.

Because we know ourselves from the inside, we are painfully aware of everything that is a bit silly and sad about being us. But when it comes to judging other people, we can only go on what they tell us — and what they tell us is a heavily edited version of the truth. The answer is, as ever, that we have to imagine information that we have not been given. We have to imagine the sadness of the perfect-seeming princess on her holiday, the doubts of the sure-looking windsurfer, the worries of the confident-seeming politician and the pimples of the apparently flawless beauty.

You're not sad or unimpressive, even if that's how looking online makes you feel. All of us are unimpressive close up — and that's fine. It's what being human means. It's important not to mistake people's stories of who they are for what they actually are. Life is difficult for everyone — and the best kind of art (and online pictures) don't let us forget that. If ever you start posting pictures of your life online, be sure to include one of your mother looking cross on holiday (even if there are palm trees) and one of your bedroom before you have tidied it. That might help other people a lot.

CHAPTER 3

Bullies

How someone becomes a bully

Sometimes other people upset us by accident. They might bump into us or they say something that hurts us, but they're not setting out to make us unhappy. But with a bully it's different: a bully wants us to feel miserable. You might be happily doing something on your own and a bully comes up and says something horrible, just to make you feel bad.

In this section we are only going to be talking about bullies who say mean things. There is another kind of bully who can be physically threatening. Physical danger is something you have to talk to a grown-up about — as is the worst kind of verbal danger too.

Let's ask a difficult question: why does the bully say mean things? Why do they want to upset other people?

The answer is surprising: *the bully is frightened*. This can be hard to believe, because a bullying person doesn't look scared or frightened. Sometimes they look as if they aren't scared of anything. In fact, they are scared of something quite specific: they are mean to others because they are scared that someone will be mean to them.

The bully is attacking in someone else the thing they are afraid of being bullied for themselves — maybe not by anyone at school, but by someone important in their life: a parent or an older brother or sister, maybe. You can't see the other parts of the bully's life. Sadly, they have probably been humiliated and harshly criticised for exactly the same kind of things they are mean to others about. The bully is being really horrible. But it's sad for them. Someone becomes a bully because they have been bullied. They responded to it by thinking, 'If I become a bully I won't be bullied.'

If you have ever felt tempted to bully someone — and nearly everyone has at some point — try to remember how you felt at the time. Why did you want to be mean to that person? What was it about them? In what way might you once have been like them? Who wasn't very nice to you?

Why people bully

Around bullying we're meeting a big idea about why people behave badly.

People are horrible
because they're suffering

People behave badly — they get angry or they do and say mean things — when they are afraid of something. Usually you can't see what they are afraid of and they don't tell you. They feel they can't explain their fear, and they are worried that if they tried to explain no one would understand. So they cover up their fears. They try to look as if they aren't afraid at all. Maybe this happens to you sometimes.

There's an old story about this. Once, a very long time ago in Egypt, there was a boy called Androcles. He lived in a village. Every night, all the people in the village could hear a lion roaring not far away in the desert. The lion sounded angry; sometimes the lion would approach the village walls and in the moonlight they could see it stretching out its sharp claws and baring its huge teeth. It looked mean and horrible.

One day, Androcles was playing near some caves and it started to rain. He went to shelter in a cave. It would have been a good place to stay dry... except there, lying at the back, was the lion. As soon as it saw Androcles, the lion jumped up and started making a terrible noise. Androcles was terrified. But, now he was close, he realised there was something strange about the noise the lion was making. It was almost as if the lion was crying. Then Androcles noticed that there was a big thorn sticking into the lion's paw. That was what had been making the lion so angry: it was in pain. It had been suffering for a long time, but it could never tell anyone what was wrong and it didn't know how to get the thorn out on its own. Quietly, Androcles went up to the lion and gently pulled out the thorn. The lion stopped roaring and lay down quietly and became the boy's friend.

It's only a story — obviously it would be a bad idea to try to take a thorn out of a lion's paw — but it makes an important point. Lots of people are like this lion. They shout or they get angry, they look mean and threatening, but actually they are suffering. They don't have a thorn sticking into their hand. They have a different kind of pain, in their mind rather than in their body.

Maybe they feel like no one loves them. Maybe they feel ashamed because they know they have been horrible. Maybe they are sad about something; they could be worried that they will be laughed at or that someone is going to get angry with them.

If someone is behaving badly, and not being nice, it is helpful to ask: what's the thorn in their mind? You probably won't know the answer. But imagining what the answer might be makes a big difference to how you see this person. Here's how a search for a thorn might go...

WHAT WAS THE UPSETTING THING?

WHAT MIGHT BE THE THORN?

Mum was angry and
she shouted at me

She has a very difficult
relationship with her sister

Dad won't let me spend
more time on my iPad

He's really worried about
his work right now

TRY WRITING YOUR OWN

People are sometimes horrible to people they like

It may sound strange, but sometimes bullies are mean to people that they like. They're so afraid they won't be liked back, they start to behave badly, almost as a way of showing how little they care, because caring is painful for them (it reminds them they might not be wanted).

It is uncomfortable to want something that you can't have, so sometimes we reinvent how much we ever wanted the missing element in the first place. When it becomes clear that something — it could be a toy, a friend, a holiday — can never be ours, we re-evaluate how much it means to us. It takes strength to hold on to the idea that something might be precious and yet out of our reach.

Imagine being 9 and entering a class at the start of the year when you notice an extraordinary new pupil: taller than you, with nice eyes, cool clothes and an intelligent smile. They're one of the most charming people you have ever encountered. They are also out of your league. You might long to become their friend. You might want to share jokes and chit-chat, but this kind of attempt could also hurt. So, to reduce the pain, you might decide you do not care. To show you don't care — to yourself and to the person you like — you become a bit nasty. You try to spoil what you cannot have. You become mean where you would, at one level, have wanted to be sweet. You call them a stuck-up idiot and worse, you organise a group to torment them; you steal their scarf. It sounds odd, but it can happen to us all.

So the next time that you find someone being mysteriously mean to you, without any arrogance, keep one thought in mind: maybe they want to be your friend and they're just scared you won't want to be friends with them.

Gossip

One of the more horrible things about living around other people is the fact that they may gossip about you — in other words, say mean things about you behind your back. Probably it's already happened to you before; it goes on a lot.

One thing to bear in mind is that not all gossip hurts equally badly. If you heard that someone had gossiped that you spent your holidays in Outer Mongolia and your family were shepherds who lived in a yurt (a kind of tent) out there, you'd think that was ridiculous. The gossip wouldn't get to you; you might laugh, because you know you were born in the local hospital and that your mum works for the government (let's say).

That tells us something important: if you know that something isn't true, even if people gossip about it, you don't mind so much.

The things we really mind being gossiped about are things that we're not sure about in ourselves. For example, if we are worried that we're no good at sports, or that our nose is too big, then if others gossip about these topics, we will feel especially wounded. Gossip gets in the cracks created by our own doubts about ourselves.

So one important way to protect ourselves from gossip is to:

Get to know ourselves better
than, and ahead of, other people

We need to develop a robust and independent way of thinking about our ability at sport or the size of our nose and a hundred other things too. One that says, 'This is how I am and I'm OK'. Even if we aren't great at sport and our nose isn't the prettiest, that doesn't matter as much as getting a solid, accurate grasp in our own heads about their true nature, so that the words of others will lose their power to hurt us.

If you really know yourself, the next time someone gossips about you, it won't be pleasant, but it won't be news to you either. You'll have gossiped enough about yourself to yourself — and so a few extra layers of gossip won't matter too much. You will know yourself better than anyone who might have anything mean to say about you. When they say a mean thing, just shrug your shoulders and say, 'Do you think that's news to me?!'

CHAPTER 4

How Old Am I?

It sounds like the easiest question in the world. Of course you know what age you are! But there's another important way in which you are actually lots of different ages all at the same time — and that's OK. There's a part of you that is still 1 and another bit of you that's 4 and three-quarters. Being happy and at peace with yourself means making friends with the idea that all the old bits of you are still in you somewhere and you can, every now and then, hang out with them.

That might sound crazy at first. But to try to make sense of this idea, let's look at a Russian doll. If you ask what size the doll is, there is not one simple answer. When all the dolls are stacked inside each other, you might think the doll is quite big. But if you could see inside you'd realise it's made up of several dolls: there's a tiny baby one, then some slightly bigger ones, and then the biggest one on the outside. So the doll is lots of different sizes at the same time.

When it comes to age, we are a bit like Russian dolls. You can't see the younger versions of yourself, but in a special way they still exist, hidden inside you.

I suck my thumb
(and my toes and
my plastic fish)

I still like to suck
my thumb

At school I miss
my mummy

Sometimes I need to
be carried by Mum

I hold hands when
I cross the road

I get carried a lot
by my parents

I *really* love
toasted fingers

Animal pasta is
the best food ever

My favourite
food is milk

Can you touch the
moon if you climb
up a big ladder?

Reading is
really hard

I'm excited by bin
trucks and cranes!

A lot of the time the younger parts of you keep quiet; you could nearly forget they are there. If you know the Moon is a lump of rock orbiting the Earth, you might think it's silly to think you could climb a ladder to reach it; but maybe another part of you remembers thinking that and it didn't feel silly at the time. If you can swim, you sort of forget how hard it was to learn, but there's a part of you that remembers feeling that you'd never be able to swim. Maybe when you're at school you don't miss your parents at all but another part of you can remember crying when your parents left in the morning. You might still feel that way some mornings.

It is OK to
be babyish

There's a terrible fear in all of us about being 'still a baby'. But maybe we could be a bit braver around this and accept the baby bit of us with greater calm. The baby isn't going to take you over, you're never going back to being tiny, so you can afford occasionally to look inside and have a shared moment with the baby-you.

It's exciting getting older; there are so many more things you can do. But sometimes a secret part of your brain does think it would be good to be little again. That can happen if you feel lonely or if you wake up in the middle of the night or if you cut your knee and it's sore. If you are tired you might feel it would be nice if a parent would pick you up and carry you; it could be nice to suck your thumb. Some people get worried by these feelings. They say that's being 'babyish'. They think that if you feel little then you can't be big as well. But the Russian doll shows that's not right. The big parts of you don't disappear just because you feel little for a while.

More about bullies

Remember we were saying that bullies are secretly afraid? Now we can understand more of what they are afraid of. If someone has been told it's not OK to be little, then they get angry with the little parts of themselves and those of others too. It looks as if they are being mean to other people, but really they are being mean to themselves. If they say: 'You are stupid, you miss your mummy', they are speaking to themselves; they are saying 'I'm frightened of the part of me that misses my mummy'.

It's still annoying if someone bullies you, but it helps if you know they are using you to attack a part of themselves.

Grown-ups can (sometimes) understand children

Grown-ups don't do the same things as children: they go to work, they drive cars, they have credit cards and talk about politics. So it sometimes feels as if they can't understand what it's like to be 9 or 11.

However, the Russian doll says that inside a grown-up there is a 9-year-old and an 11-year-old. Maybe they used to fret about their projects on what happens inside a volcano, or worry if their handwriting wasn't neat, or get worried about who they would play with during the breaks at school, or felt it was unfair they had to go to bed early when the grown-ups stayed up late, or spent a lot of time thinking about what a new babysitter would be like. All these feelings are still there. So even though a grown-up looks very different from you, they might still understand a lot about what is happening in your life.

CHAPTER 5

School

A little bit of history

You spend a huge part of your life at school, thinking about school and doing things connected to school. It goes on for a very long time. School is so familiar, it's hard to realise that the kind of school you know is a recent invention. For most of human history, hardly anyone went to school; very few people could read or write. Mostly, children were educated to do a specific job.

In this era, children would train in the workshop of a famous artist

Philip Galle, *A Painter's Workshop*, c.1595

If you wanted to be an artist, at the age of about 8 or 9 you would go and work alongside an adult artist (standing on the platform in the middle and wearing an interesting hat). It's tricky to spot the children in this picture because they are wearing the same type of clothes as the grown-ups.

Or, if you lived on a farm — which was where most people lived — you would probably start working full-time looking after the animals when you were still very young.

James Guthrie, *To Pastures New*, 1883

At one time, most people lived on farms and helped with the work when they were children

If someone did go to school, it would only be for a few years — maybe from when they were 8 until they were 12. Often they did not learn very much.

Schools today are mostly a lot better, but they're not perfect yet. That's not surprising. Grown-ups still aren't sure how a school should be organised, what you need to learn and what the best ways of teaching those things might be. When you think about how different education has been in the past it helps you realise that it could be very different in the future as well. No wonder, on some days, you think your school could be a lot better. It probably could. Human beings are still working school out!

What is education?

At first you might think education is just another name for what happens at school. Actually, the idea of education is much bigger. Education means learning things. But what kinds of things can we learn?

Think of a stand-up comic. They don't magically know how to make funny jokes; they have to learn, but they probably had to teach themselves. Being funny isn't something that's taught in schools, but it could be. If we were

If children did go to school they would only learn basic things like how to read and do sums

Jan Steen, *The Village School*, c. 1670

taught, not everyone would be a stand-up comic (we all learn how to write, but hardly any people are writers for their job), but everyone would be much funnier.

Or, think about the way some people are kind: they are good at getting others to join in; they're nice to you if you have a problem; if you get upset they are good at calming you down. They didn't know how to do these things when they were babies; they learned how to do them. Other people could learn as well, but 'being nice' isn't something that gets taught very much. Maybe it should be taught a lot more, because being nice is one of the things that really helps you get on in life. Often getting a good job depends on people liking you and thinking you have a nice personality. (The right qualifications do matter, but if you talk to any boss, they are always keen to have a nice person working in their company! That's not something school ever teaches you.)

Some people are good at coping with difficulties. When things go wrong, they don't get into a huge panic: they calmly work out what the least bad option is and get on with doing that. If they make a mistake they don't get too upset, they go back and see if there's anything they can do to put it right; they don't worry too much about pleasing everyone; they can feel quite good about themselves even if not everyone likes them. Are they just lucky? Actually, these are all skills that can be taught, but usually we don't get taught them very carefully.

How are we taught to respond? Probably people say things to you like: 'Calm down' or 'It does not matter that much' or 'It is OK'. This is like someone trying to teach you to read by saying: 'Read that book!' Schools know it takes years of having lessons every single day to teach someone to read. Or imagine if a teacher tried to teach you to play the piano by saying:

'Look at that person, they can play the piano, why can't you?' Learning something difficult takes a lot of time and practice and a lot of help, and learning how to react to things is no different.

There are many areas of education, but schools usually focus on just a few of them. Sometimes if you get bored at school, it's not because you hate education but because your school isn't teaching you the things you would like to learn — and indeed should learn — to have a nice life. Here are some things that people might want to know about:

Can I learn to get less upset when I lose a game?

Why is riding a bike so nice?

Why do grown-ups like coffee, beer and wine?

Why are some people nice and some people nasty?

How do people get rich?

Why was my mum in such a bad mood this morning?

Does it matter if you are in the 'cool' group?

Why do grown-ups talk about money so much?

Are there other things that would be on your own list of things you'd like to learn? It doesn't matter if you can't think of them right now. You can always come back later and add something.

Sometimes it feels awkward writing down what you are really interested in. It's fine just to think it. The important thing is that you are thinking about what you want to learn — and maybe it's not being taught. If you were inventing the ideal school for you, what would it be like?

School gives a misleading idea of success in later life

At school you tend to be aware of who is doing well and who isn't. Some people get great marks in tests, others do badly. If you are struggling at school, you might start to worry. In particular, you might worry this means you're going to have a hard time when you are grown up. But how much does school matter for the rest of your life? Let's think about this quite carefully. There are two very important things we can see when we look at people's lives:

FACT 1
There are people who do well at school but don't have much success in life. Of course, doing well at school does not stop you doing well later! It's just that not everyone who excels at school does well afterwards when they are grown-ups.

Let's look at some of the things that help people to do well *after* school. To get on well as an adult, it's useful to be:

Sensitive to the needs of other people

Able to admit when you might be wrong

Able to calm down upset or angry people

Able to stick up for good ideas when necessary

Interested in ideas (even from people you don't like)

Good at helping other people in need

Nice to people that you don't like very much

Able to lead without seeming really bossy

All these things are helpful when it comes to being a successful adult. They help with doing well at a job or enjoying your life or being married. But school tests and exams do not check on any of these things. So you can not tell from someone's exam results, or whether they are good at spelling or maths or did a great project on the Egyptian pyramids, how they might get on later in life.

Another big difference between school and the rest of life is this — in a school test, *someone already knows the answer*. Your teacher knows how to spell 'theatre', can divide 3,983 by 17, and can draw a clear picture of how a volcano works; in the test they want to find out if you know these things as well. At school you are learning things that lots of older people know already.

There is an unfortunate thing that can happen. After years at school, people come to think that *all* the important questions in life will be like questions in a school test. But later in life you often have to face questions that no one really knows the answer to, such as:

Is it really a good idea to build a new factory?

What should be on the menu at a restaurant?

How do you make up a really funny joke?

What should the price of a bunch of flowers be?

Throughout your whole life, there will be lots of important questions that only you can know the answer to:

What makes you feel happy? Why?

What do you think is important? Why?

Who do you want to be friends with?

What interests you? What is your passion?

For these questions, there isn't a teacher who already knows the right answers. Being good at tests and exams doesn't show you'll be good at answering these kinds of questions, and being bad at tests and exams doesn't mean you'll be bad at answering them.

When you are at school it can feel important to do well. But doing well at school isn't very much like doing well when you are older. Success in later life isn't the same as success at school. The two kinds of success are based on different things, so you can't tell how later life will go from how things are going at school. All the possibilities remain open. Doing badly at school doesn't mean you will definitely do well later. But doing badly at school absolutely doesn't stop you doing well later. Doing well at school certainly doesn't stop you doing well later. But doing well at school doesn't mean you'll definitely do well later.

Wanting to do everything right

Some children want to be good at school. Maybe you sometimes feel like this. If you have homework, you want to get it all right and make sure your writing is perfect. If there's a test, you hate it if you make any mistakes. Perhaps you are careful not to do anything you are not supposed to do (and maybe you get upset if others sometimes break the rules); you want the teachers to be pleased with you and you'd get worried if they weren't pleased with you.

You might think: 'Isn't that what you are supposed to do?' Actually, there are some problems with always trying to be good.

> You might make many mistakes
> before you get something right

On the next page is an example of work done by a famous writer. Imagine that your homework looked like this — full of crossing-outs and changes. It looks messy! Then they made even more changes. Eventually, they got it the way they wanted it, but it took a long time. If they'd thrown it away because it was all wrong they'd never have been able to improve it later.

SOMETIMES YOU HAVE TO DISAPPOINT SOME PEOPLE

Not all good people agree about everything: in fact, they often disagree about a lot of things. If you want to say something that's important to you,

you'll find that some people won't like it (though some others probably will agree with you). If you try hard to please everyone who is in a position of authority, you won't be able to say or do things that are important to you and are really worth doing. Anything that is worth being loyal to will be met with some opposition and disapproval, and will upset at least a few people.

YOU CAN BE CARED FOR AND APPRECIATED EVEN IF YOU MAKE MISTAKES

At the very back of your mind there might be a worry that unless you get everything right a teacher or a parent won't admire you or like you or want to look after you and help you. But actually all grown-ups have made lots of mistakes in their lives — everyone has.

Genuine kindness will include understanding mistakes, failings and imperfections. You should be careful not to put too much hope in people who won't allow you to make a mistake. They might be kind people deep down, but that's not a kind way to behave to anyone.

CHAPTER 6

Friends

What is a friend?

This is a pretty unusual question, but an important one. You might call someone a friend, but what does 'friend' actually mean?

Usually, we might think of a friend as someone we spend time with, who likes some of the things we do and who we can chat to. That's nice, but there are other things a friend might do. What does a really good friend actually do? Probably some of the things on the next page.

This list explains why you might not have a lot of friends — or even no really, really good friends. Here's a secret:

Many people don't
have very good friends

They have people they hang out with and pass the time with. But these aren't amazing friends. They're just how you cope with who is available.

Here's a thought that an ancient philosopher called Seneca once said, 'A true friend is as rare as a comet in the sky.' Comets sometimes only come along once every fifty years, so that is rare!

To recognise a good friend, there are a few traits that you can look out for.

If you say you're feeling worried to a good friend, they don't say, 'It doesn't matter at all, don't be silly'; instead they will say, 'Tell me what you are worried about'. When you are telling them something, they'll listen and say, 'That's interesting, tell me more'. If you've made a mistake they will admit they've made mistakes as well. They'll tell you their own mistakes, saying, 'I was stupid, I was a bit scared, I messed up.' They let you see the vulnerable parts of them and they quietly invite you to share your troubles with them. A good friend might upset you sometimes, but if they do they are genuinely sorry and they tell you they are.

Acknowledges your feelings (even bad ones)

Listens and is interested to know more

Apologises and will genuinely be sorry

Shares their vulnerabilities with you

Enjoys hearing about the secret bits of you

Makes you feel normal if you've made a mistake

Remember a little while ago we were talking about what makes you 'you'? All the funny things that go through your head when you're brushing your teeth? Well, a good friend is curious about that stuff. They might even be curious about who you were when you were 1 or 6. It's quite difficult (and very special) to be a good friend. It might be that you haven't met your great friend yet — they come along all through your life.

In the meantime, you might feel lonely sometimes. Lots of people are lonely, even though they don't seem it and have lots of people they hang out with day to day. There's nothing 'weird' or 'sad' about being lonely. It's often a sign that you are a complicated and interesting person. Some of the people who made this book also feel lonely, though you might not think so if you only saw them from the outside.

Being a friend to yourself

How friendly are you to yourself? It's a strange question and it's tricky to answer. So let's try an experiment.

Imagine that someone in your class is eating their lunch and they have a bit of tomato stuck to their chin. What sorts of things would the nicest friend say? They might say something like: 'You've got a sweet little bit of tomato hiding on your chin. I'm always getting things on my face when I eat.' They make the situation OK and even fun. An unfriendly person might say: 'That's so embarrassing! You look ridiculous; you don't even know how to eat properly, you can't get anything right. You baby!'

Now imagine it's you. You suddenly realise you've got a bit of tomato on your face. What do you tell yourself? Maybe you think, 'I'm so ridiculous, I don't even know how to eat properly, I can't do anything right.' It is a bit strange to think of it, but you are being mean to yourself. If you were a good friend to yourself, you might think the same sorts of things a nice person would think: 'This could happen to anyone; it actually looks quite funny. Good old me with my tomato chin!'

Try to catch the thoughts that go through your head. They will tell you if you're being a friend to yourself or if you are being unfriendly to yourself.

Let's look at another example: suppose someone at school really wanted to be in a sports team but they weren't picked. What would an unfriendly person say? Maybe something like this: 'You're no good, you'll never be picked, you try and try but you are just a failure, you always have been and you always will be.' Now think about what the nicest friend might say, something like: 'That's bad luck, I know it's a big disappointment, but you nearly got in, and you're trying really hard and that's great. Not getting into the team doesn't change how I think about you; I like you anyway; let's go and do something interesting.'

Suppose it was you who didn't get into the team. What kinds of things might you say to yourself? Would they be more like the unfriendly person or the nice person?

To get a picture of how friendly (or not) you are to yourself, try filling in the blank spaces on the next page. After you have filled out the spaces, take a close look at what you would say to yourself and ask, 'Am I being a good friend to myself?' If you see that quite often you are not a very good friend to yourself, that's actually normal. Most of us aren't as nice to ourselves as we are to other people.

HOW DO YOU GET TO BE A BETTER FRIEND TO YOURSELF?

Once you notice you're not being nice to yourself, you can deliberately change the way you speak inside your own head. You already know how to: you can imagine what a good friend would say when things go wrong.

So when you are feeling worried or upset, or if you think you have done something stupid, you can ask yourself, 'What would a nice person say to me now?'

If you try to do this regularly, it will start to become a habit. You'll find you automatically say friendly things to yourself, and life will get a lot sweeter.

If someone did rather badly in a test at school

WHAT WOULD A NICE
FRIEND SAY?

WHAT WOULD I SAY
TO MYSELF?

If someone spilled some orange juice on the carpet

WHAT WOULD A NICE
FRIEND SAY?

WHAT WOULD I SAY
TO MYSELF?

If someone was not feeling well on their birthday

WHAT WOULD A NICE
FRIEND SAY?

WHAT WOULD I SAY
TO MYSELF?

Envy

Some people have things you haven't got, but you would like to have — or maybe they are good at some things and you're not, but you wish you were. It can be annoying to think about these people. Here are some examples of envious feelings:

They are going on a ski holiday and I have to stay at home

Their parents let them spend loads of time on their computer

I wish I looked less like me and more like them

Their family has a really nice car and mine doesn't

They are skilled at playing sport and I'm not very good

They are good at maths and I struggle

Imagine you admit you feel envy. A lot of people would say, 'You shouldn't feel that. It's not good to feel envy. It's not nice. You should appreciate what you have already and not worry about what other people have or can do.' It is quite good advice. But there's another unusual approach that might be more helpful. It involves thinking seriously and carefully about envy. Instead of *trying not to feel envy*, the idea is to ask envy some interesting questions. Maybe envy has something important to tell you?

Here's another way to think about it. Do you know about radar? It is used at airports to detect incoming planes. It's a very clever invention, but it's limited in what it can say. If you were looking at it, it might suddenly make a beeping noise. It's picked up on something approaching. But what is it? The radar machine can't tell you. It might be a tiny plane; it might be a huge plane. You have to ask some more questions. You might need to make radio contact and speak to the pilot. Radar is a fantastic invention: it tells you something, but it doesn't tell you everything you need to know.

Envy is like this. It tells you that there's something about this other person that's important to you. But it doesn't tell you exactly what. You might think it is obvious, but perhaps it isn't. Perhaps you envy the ski holiday. But what is it that you would really like? Maybe it's not so much skiing; it's the idea of doing something interesting with your dad. Maybe, once you start to think about it, you don't so much want to go skiing as hang out more with your father, which you haven't been able to do since he moved out.

Or what about envying a nice car? Ask yourself what it is about the car that seems so appealing. It does look great, but when you think about it, what really excites you about it is that if your mum was driving that car she'd be very happy. And she hasn't been very happy lately. She complains a lot about things, and you don't really know what to do to help her.

What this is telling you is that it is not actually the ski trip or the car that is important to you. There are other things that skiing and the car are pointing to that matter more.

Or maybe you envy someone who is good at maths. What is it you actually wish for in yourself? The first radar answer is 'being good at maths.' But what's really behind that? Maybe you want to be admired or appreciated. Maybe you know how much your parents admire maths and, also, how tough they are with you sometimes, telling you that you don't do enough around the house and are lazy.

If you think about it, what you really envy isn't maths, but people who feel cosy around their parents. You've met an even more important idea through envying someone's ability to do some hard sums and equations. But actually what you are concerned about has not really got anything much to do with maths.

What you envy sends you a mixed-up but interesting signal about who you want to be. But because it's mixed up it might give you the wrong idea. It might make you think, 'I need to go skiing', when really you want to have more fun with your parents. Or it makes you think you have to be good at maths, when really you just want to be better appreciated for something, like being you.

What's interesting is that the thing you really want might be more easily available to you than the thing you envy. Maybe you just can't go skiing, but you could play a game with your dad. Maybe your mum won't get a fancy car, but you could try to cheer her up by curling up under a blanket with her on the sofa and watching TV.

As an exercise, try writing down the names of some people you envy. Then say what it is you envy them for. Then take a good long think. What's the really appealing thing here? Not the obvious thing, but the things that are lying behind it? How could you get more of that thing in your life?

Shyness

Imagine you saw a lamb and it looked sweet and you wanted to go up to it and give it a handful of delicious grass. However, as soon as it saw you approaching, it would run away. Why does the lamb do this? The reason is: it thinks you're a threat, even though you're not. You could say the lamb is shy because it's acting like shy people do.

Maybe you feel shy sometimes; that is understandable. When you see a new person you don't know, your brain sends out a 'danger' signal, even though this person might actually be nice. It could be when a good friend of your parents comes round for dinner and your parents ask you to say hello and you feel like running away and hiding behind the curtains; or perhaps if there's a new person in your class at school you feel you can't talk to them.

Just as with the lamb, your brain might be making a mistake. You think this person is a threat, but actually they could be very nice. The alarm bells in your head are not always good at telling the difference between a nice person and a not so nice one.

To make sense of this, think about a fire alarm. Fire alarms are a very good idea — you want to be alerted if a real fire starts. But you can imagine a fire alarm that's so sensitive that it goes off even if you are just boiling some water to make pasta: it can't tell the difference between steam and an actual fire. It could be going off a lot, even when there's no danger at all.

A shy person's brain is like an over-sensitive fire alarm. Around other people, there can occasionally be danger and so we want an alarm that tells us about that. But we can understand the big idea that the alarm might be too sensitive and goes off too quickly, even when there is no danger at all.

Let's think about the kinds of people who might make you feel shy. They are probably people who are not obviously like you. They might be older or younger; their hair might look more messy or neater than yours; they might have a different way of speaking; they might wear smart clothes or have funny shoes. Your brain is saying: if someone looks like that they can't be friendly, but often they are actually good-natured and kind.

Something that helps with shyness is to imagine the rest of someone's life. They might not look like you but there could be lots of things about them that mean they will understand you and be friendly towards you.

WHAT IS IT ABOUT THEM THAT MAKES YOU FEEL SHY?	WHAT ELSE MIGHT BE TRUE FOR THEM?
They are big; they are wearing a green shirt; they are old	Their child is your age; they remember being young; they are quite shy sometimes
They are really good at games and you aren't very good	Their brother or sister, who they like very much, is not at all good at games either
They are a child who is visiting from a far away country	They have a friend who is a bit like you at home; they're worried no one likes them
They have a lot of money when you don't have much at all	They don't think money is everything; they're embarrassed when they have new things
They look a bit tough; they look grumpy and do not say hello	They're actually thoughtful and gentle; they are feeling a bit shy… just like you!

The point is, there's usually a lot more going on in someone's mind than is obvious from the way they look. How they look doesn't tell you much about who they are. But the alarm bell in your head is ringing anyway. Learn to ignore it, like your mother does with the fire alarm when the toaster sets it off by accident.

To help with shyness there are some questions you can ask yourself. The first one is: *who makes me feel shy?*

It sounds easy, but maybe it's not. It is a strangely big step sometimes just to tell yourself something. The second question is: *what's my worry about them?*

Maybe you think they'll laugh at you or say something mean or ignore you. Maybe you feel that because of what they're like, they couldn't be nice to you. They're too smart or too messy or too old or too pretty or too noisy or too clever or too young. It could be so many things: their face reminds you of someone you don't like; they come from a place you don't know; they look serious...

Then you can ask yourself the most important question:

What else could I imagine
about them that would help?

There's a strangely helpful idea to keep in mind: we are all very similar underneath our differences.

The secret of true love

Every so often you might hear people talk about 'love' in a slightly giggly way. Maybe they say someone at school loves someone else; or maybe there is a film in which someone says 'I love you'. Maybe some older people you know are going to get married and someone says they are getting married because they love each other. It sounds funny and a bit puzzling.

So what is love? Loving someone, in the sense of being very kind to them, can mean:

You are interested in their problems and want to understand them properly

You keep on being friendly to them, even if they aren't very nice for a while

You do something they like, because they want to, even if it's not your first choice

You always want what is best for them

Their happiness is as important to you as your own

You tell them when they are making a mistake, even if they're annoyed, because you want to help them

Imagine someone felt this way about you: it would be great. It's the way parents normally feel about their children. They don't always get it right, but it is usually what they are trying to do. So you do know what love is — because you've been loved. This is the big, important kind of love that everyone wants and that all good adult relationships involve, to some degree. So although other people might giggle about who's in love with who, it isn't because they *know* what love is, but because they've *forgotten*.

How to make a true friend

There are lots of different ways to make friends: you might have the same interests as them, you might know their parents, you might go on holiday with them... But here's a way that we especially like:

Tell them something
unexpected about yourself

By something unexpected, we mean something that only a few people know about you (or perhaps none at all) — something you think makes you a little bit unusual. For example, that you dislike a certain teacher; or that you quite enjoy maths homework; or that you're jealous of a girl in class.

You might start with a fact about yourself (I hate changing for PE; I think the school toilets are scary; football is boring...) and choose someone you always get on well with, who is kind, to tell it to. If they respond nicely, you can tell them more. By giving a friend this information about you, what you're really saying is:

> I trust you with a precious
> part of myself

You are giving them a special bit of knowledge about yourself that you wouldn't give to many other people, because you believe that they're the kind of person who you can confide in.

And because your new friend will feel that you've given them this lovely present — an unexpected fact about you — they are likely to feel safe enough about doing the same back. They may tell you something unusual about themselves. They may tell you that they're scared of dogs, or that they're allergic to fish, or that they can turn their eyelids inside out. These unusual facts act like a kind of glue — they are what makes friendship stick. It's hard to be a really great friend of someone who doesn't know any of your secret, weird or particular parts. And you can make sure to take care of their secrets just like they will take care of yours.

We might think that, in order to make friends, we always need to be cool, mysterious and tough. That is true in some cases, but if we are talking about real friendship, then the only way to make a proper friend is to take a risk with a unique part of you. It should be worth it in the end.

CHAPTER 7

Your Body

Your body and your brain

Your brain is where your thoughts and feelings happen — but, crucially, your brain is also part of your body. This means that what happens in your body will — and this can sound odd — impact on your ideas and views on things.

With babies this can be pretty obvious. A 1-year-old can be smiling and gurgling and playing happily with a yellow plastic cup and then quite quickly they throw the cup away and start crying. A grown-up might say something like: 'Oh, she's getting tired, she needs a nap'; or 'She must be getting hungry'. The baby's mood changes *because of what's happening in the rest of her body*.

This continues right across the whole of our lives. Lots of things about our bodies can influence our moods, like not getting enough sunshine or enough sleep at night, not drinking enough water or the right kind of food, or even just spending a long time sitting down. Perhaps your body might feel too hot or too cold, and that is changing your mood.

When these things happen we might feel upset. We get irritated, we get annoyed with people, we feel everything is too difficult. When you think about it, this makes sense. What is happening in your brain depends on the state of your body, so if something's going wrong for your body it's not surprising it affects your mind.

But there's often a tricky thing here: our brains don't tell us *when* and *why* they are getting in a bad mood. Our brains don't send a signal saying: 'Watch out, I'm getting gloomy because I'm getting tired. I'm probably going to start getting annoyed with Mum in about two minutes because

I'm low on vitamins'. Or 'Hang on, I'm dehydrated, so I'm about to feel I can't do my work and that school is unfair and horrible'.

You simply get cross and bothered, but you don't see the real reason for it. You blame Mum or school, but the real reason you are in a bad mood isn't to do with Mum or school, it's because of a problem with your body.

We hear a lot about why we need to keep our bodies in a healthy state (this isn't the mission of this book). But here's something else to think about: our bodies have a habit of not telling us how much they play with our minds. The next time you think you hate everyone and your parents are awful and the dog is mean too, ask yourself a few simple questions:

Did I get enough sleep last night?

Have I drunk enough water today?

Should I stop spending so much time on the iPad?

Do I need to stop eating so much chocolate?

It's no insult to our big brains to remember that they need good food, sleep and exercise to work well. Maybe you hate exercise, and fruit and vegetables too: so be it. But because you love your mind, for its sake, take a few moments every day to look after your body.

I don't like how I look

Perhaps you know the feeling. Maybe you look in the mirror and worry that your arms are too thin or you wish your chin was different. Or maybe you get self-conscious: you spend a lot of the day worrying that your hair doesn't look great or you think people are laughing at you because you've got big feet.

It is pretty normal. Lots of people have these worries, even people that you would not expect. Many people think that this actress was the most beautiful person in the world. But she did not like the way she looked. She worried every single day about the shape of her nose.

Lots of people think that Marilyn Monroe is beautiful, but she didn't like how she looked

So let's ask an unusual question: *why* do we worry about how we look?

Probably it is because we think that other people will judge us on our looks. They are going to concentrate on the colour of our hair or the shape of our legs or whether we have a pimple on our forehead.

It's not surprising if we feel this: our society does comment a lot on how people look. Adverts show us pictures of good-looking people and suggest that what you look like is the most important thing about you. We can easily feel that we shouldn't like ourselves because of how we look.

One way of dealing with this is to try to change how we look: some people do special exercises to flatten their stomach muscles or build up their shoulders. And some adults might get a doctor to change the shape of their mouth or nose. But something that might be more useful, which is more to do with your mind, is the idea that:

Your body
is not you

In the past, people used to talk about the 'soul'. What they meant by 'soul' was your personality, your thoughts and feelings. They made a big distinction between the soul and the body. In particular, they said that the soul was more important than the body. You could have an interesting soul even if your body wasn't special, and you could have a not-very-nice soul even if your body was lovely. They made lots of paintings to remind themselves of this idea.

This picture suggests that a person's soul can be nice even if they have a bit of a funny nose

Domenico Ghirlandaio, *An Old Man and his Grandson*, c. 1490

This picture says: this person is really kind, even though they have an ordinary face

Rembrandt van Rijn, *Hendrickje Stoffels*, mid-1650s

The message of these paintings was: it's more important what your soul is like than what your body or your face is like. You are not your body. You are your soul.

These pictures come from long ago, but what they are saying is still very important. Any odd person can have a decent body; only a few wonderful people can have a great soul. And that person might be you.

My body is changing

Perhaps there are older children you've known for a few years. They used to be like you and now they have changed. They have got hairy legs or a different voice; maybe they have got some spots on their face; they are suddenly taller or the whole shape of their body is changing.

When this happens varies quite a lot, but mostly it takes place somewhere between the ages of about 10 and 16. It can look pretty alarming. Maybe you don't want your body to change. Maybe it's started already.

A big, secret worry might be: if my body changes, will I have to become someone else? If someone starts to look different, does it mean they are becoming a different person? Will I stop being me?

Your body is changing all the time; so is everyone else's. Four years ago you were probably a different size. Maybe your hair was a slightly different colour. Maybe you had a gap where you were waiting for your front teeth to come in. Probably your face has changed quite a bit. Have you become a different person?

A good way of putting it might be to say: *you have become more you*. It's not that you have stopped being the person you were four years ago. Rather, you have added to that person and you have extended and developed who you are.

Imagine you could take a photo of someone on the same day every year, starting before their 1st birthday and going on until they were 80 or maybe even 100 years old. You'd see a little change every single year. Over five or ten years you would notice quite big changes. Over twenty years it would be huge.

What's going to happen in the next few years isn't actually strange; it's just the same as what's been happening up till now. The key thing is that you won't stop being you. Your soul will carry on, whatever your body is doing. Or, to describe it another way: the car you're travelling in might change, but you will still be the passenger.

Gender

It's quite odd when you think about it: there are billions of people in the world and they are generally split into just two groups: boys and girls, or men and women.

We're made to feel that it really matters which group we're in. If you're on the female side or the male side it's supposed to make a big difference. That's odd, because if there are billions of any kind of person obviously there will be billions of variations. There are going to be lots of different ways of being female or male. So knowing whether someone is female or male might not tell you much about them.

So here is a big conclusion:

Gender doesn't say what
you are supposed to be like

Over the centuries in different countries, ideas about what girls or boys are 'meant' to be like have changed a lot. If you were a boy and you lived in England around 1630 (and were well off) you'd be expected to grow your hair long, wear high-heeled shoes, lots of lace, and a huge floppy hat.

You would have had special lessons in how to make elegant gestures with your hands as you bowed or waved to someone. If you didn't, your parents would complain and other people would make jokes behind your back.

Or, going back even further, if you were a girl and you lived in Athens, Greece around 400 BC, you'd only be taught how to do things like cooking and weaving, and you would not be allowed to grow up to become a poet, politician or an artist (even though plenty of girls would have been very good at these jobs). If you were a boy, you'd be expected to learn about law and the military and not about sewing clothes or organising a cupboard, even though you might have preferred doing these things.

Societies in the past were quite strict at having rules about what you were supposed to like or want to be. It meant that a lot of people didn't get to do things they'd have been good at and that they'd have enjoyed.

Today, we do not have such strict rules, but we do have something not entirely different: expectations based around averages. It goes like this:

Girls are supposed to love flowers, but boys aren't supposed to pay any attention to them

Girls are expected to care a lot about what they wear, but boys are not supposed to care about fashion

Boys are presumed to be really interested in racing fast cars, but girls are supposed to only be interested in the car's colour

Many people think boys play ball sports all the time, and that girls dislike games and stay clear of them

Because this is such an important question, we are going to get a little bit technical. Let's get quite serious about what averages actually are. Suppose we ask, do girls like cars? How would we find out? We'd have to ask all the girls there are. The answer would probably look like this...

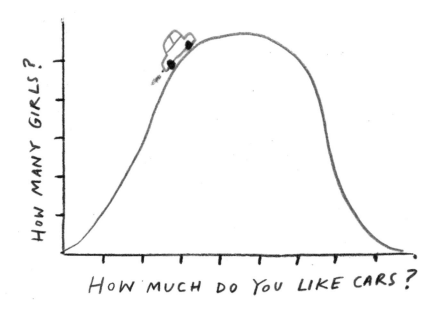

It's just as you'd imagine: there's a huge spread of every possible attitude Some girls really hate cars, some love them, and most are somewhere in between. If we asked boys, we would get the same spread, but a few more would be on the 'pretty interested' side.

But you can see something quite amazing: in spite of the average, some girls like cars a lot and some boys don't like them at all. So, what boys or girls *usually* do or like isn't much of a guide to what *you* should do or like. It can seem as if whether you are a girl or a boy is the most important thing in saying who you are. But that's not true. There are lots and lots of things that make you who you are that aren't connected to being a girl or a boy. Here's a list of questions that help say who you are:

Where do you like to go on holiday? Beach or city?

What makes you laugh?

What would you like to learn more about?

What are some of your most favourite foods?

What makes you cry?

Do you like to teach other people or be taught?

What kind of stories are your favourite?

Would you prefer to live in the city or the country?

The answers you give to all of these questions are important for saying who you are. But none of them depend on gender. If you just knew that someone was a girl or a boy you wouldn't know much about them at all. That makes life a lot more interesting and free!

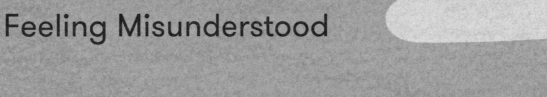

CHAPTER 8

Feeling Misunderstood

One of the biggest challenges is getting other people to understand what we mean. Ideally, when there's something going on in you, you use words to tell another person and they understand, so now they've got the same thought as you.

But a lot of the time it does not happen like this. Other people do not understand. You say some things but it doesn't seem to work. You can tell that their thought bubble isn't like yours.

When that happens, you might react in various ways. Maybe you will lose your temper; you get annoyed and feel the other person is too stupid to understand! Or you get in a bad mood: other people could understand, if they wanted to, but they are too mean! Or you might give up trying to explain and start to wonder if anyone cares what you think and feel.

The real problem is that it's difficult to get an idea that's in your head to make its way safely and reliably into the head of another person.

To get a sense of the difficulty, imagine you're speaking to someone on the phone. They can't see this picture of a teapot:

You have to describe what the teapot looks like to them. You might say something like: 'It's very pretty and decorative with an elegant handle and some very lovely details of flowers on the pot. The spout is quite tall and points upward.'

The other person has to do a drawing based on what you've said, then they send you their picture. They might do a drawing like this:

It's not much like the teapot you were describing. But it's not your fault or theirs: it's just tricky to describe it.

This kind of difficulty happens a lot. You know what you are thinking and feeling, but it is hard to say it in words. So the other person gets a slightly (or very) wrong idea of what you have in mind. It is no one's fault, it just happens!

But we can learn to get better at it. There is a special name for this skill: *teaching*. When you think about it, this is what a teacher is doing a lot of the time. There's something they know and they want you to know it too. They know how a volcano works, and how a raindrop eventually ends up in the ocean, and why Japan is in a different time zone from Mexico; their job is to get what's in their head into your head.

There are lots of things good teachers do:

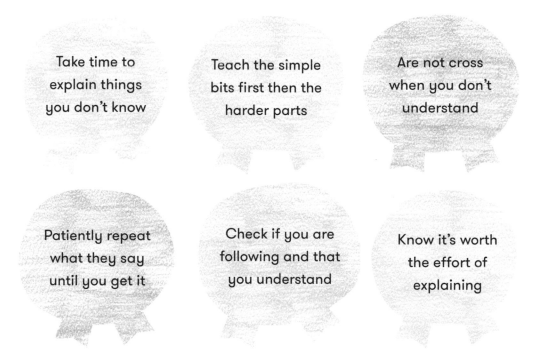

Take time to explain things you don't know

Teach the simple bits first then the harder parts

Are not cross when you don't understand

Patiently repeat what they say until you get it

Check if you are following and that you understand

Know it's worth the effort of explaining

You can understand this about teachers. Now, let's think of *you* as the teacher — not trying to teach someone about volcanoes but about your thoughts and feelings.

Imagine the picture in your head is this: you were standing talking to your friend Sally about going on a bike ride. You said you'd been on a bike ride with your dad. You didn't mention that you'd really enjoyed going on the ride, but you were thinking about that. She asked what kind of bike you have and you said it's green. And she said, 'Green isn't a kind of bike.' She said it in a special way that means: you're stupid if you think 'green' is a kind of bike. And you know, of course, that green isn't a kind of bike, but it's important to you that your bike is green, as you really like that colour. Now you feel sad because this person, who you used to quite like, was trying to make you feel silly, but you are not silly. Why do people do that?

Suppose you want to tell your mum about it. How might the conversation go? It *could* go like this:

How was school today?

Sally wasn't very nice to me

Don't worry, she probably didn't mean to be

You wouldn't understand

It feels as if your mum isn't listening and doesn't care. But if you look at what you said, it's not so surprising. The words you used didn't really give her a proper picture of what happened and why it bothered you.

Here's a different version, using teacher skills. In this version, your mum understands what was bothering you and is sympathetic. But it's not that Mum has changed. It's just that this is a way of teaching her about what happened and why it mattered.

Mum, do you remember Sally?

I think so…

She's in my class, I talk to her at break

Oh yes, I remember her

Today I talked to Sally about bike rides. You know how I liked going on that ride with Dad on Sunday

Yes, you had a great time!

I told Sally I'd been on a bike ride with Dad. Do you know what she said?

What?

She didn't ask if I'd had a nice time; she just asked me 'What kind of bike have you got?'

Mmm…

Are you not following?

Not exactly

I wanted Sally to ask about the ride with Dad and she didn't — she just asked what bike I have

So...?

I said 'green'. I wasn't thinking about my bike, I was thinking about Dad

That makes sense

She said: 'Green isn't a kind of bike. You are silly if you think that!' I feel like she wasn't very nice to me

I see, yes. That must have been a bit upsetting

If you feel that someone doesn't understand you, it's maybe not that they can't or don't want to understand. There's another possibility: it's quite tricky explaining what the matter is and as yet you do not have enough skills to get them to see what's going on in your head. But you can learn how to do it, just as you can learn other tricky things like how to swim or ride a bike. You can learn how to be a good teacher, not of the boring stuff at school, but of something far more important: a teacher of what makes you *you*.

CHAPTER 9

Anger

Getting angry is never a particularly good idea. It is not very nice to see furious toddlers, and it's no less upsetting to see adults when they start yelling uncontrollably. Probably — like all of us — you've been angry too sometimes. There's no point feeling guilty, but maybe there is a way to be calmer going forward. You may think that getting angry is just something that happens, like rain or lightning; it's a natural phenomenon that can't be stopped. But surprisingly, anger isn't some kind of inevitable bodily reaction. It's the result of certain sorts of ideas — and if we could only change some of our ideas, we could also be a lot less angry.

To get to the root of what makes us feel angry, let's begin with a basic distinction between feeling *sad* and feeling *angry*. Neither is ideal. Both are negative states, but in some ways, feeling sad is better than being angry. When you're angry, you might shout, smash things or call people an idiot. When you're sad, you might sigh, or lie down on your bed, or rest your forehead against the window and watch the clouds, or, best of all, talk to a parent, sibling or close friend about what's making you feel this way. To put it another way: it's easier to make a sad person feel better than an angry one. You might try a little exercise, filling in this table:

WHAT MAKES ME ANGRY WHAT MAKES ME SAD

One of the things to notice is that the difference between the Angry things and the Sad things has nothing to do with seriousness. You could be sad that your grandmother has died, but angry that you can't find your pencil. You could be sad that you're never going to learn the violin properly, but angry that your sister hasn't put the top back on the orange juice.

Both anger and sadness start off with frustration, with a wish that has not been fulfilled. But the frustration will make us *sad* when it is *expected*. It might make us *furious* when it is a *surprise*. You could put it like this:

Frustration
+ Surprise = Anger

Frustration
+ Expectation = Sadness

What makes us angry are frustrations, large or small, that we have not budgeted for; that we didn't expect to happen. For example, think of how you respond when it rains and you'd planned a nice day out. You're sad, no doubt, but you wouldn't start kicking the furniture.

However, imagine if you'd been looking forward to getting to your holiday destination and suddenly the pilot said that there would be a five-hour delay on the flight. Then you (or your parents) might get angry. That is because you expect that it might rain pretty much any day, but you don't expect that your aeroplane will let you down like that. We stay calm about difficult things that we expect might happen, but we can get angry when we're taken by surprise. If we want to lead a better life, it can be wise to expect a bit more and be surprised a bit less.

Another way to put it is that people who get angry often are, without really knowing it, operating with high expectations. Let's go further: they are strangely optimistic. Angry people are optimistic. They don't seem optimistic. When you see an angry person in a rage, they appear extremely dark. But they are, beneath all that, still optimistic. They have refused to expect frustration. They think everything will always go to plan. They think that trains will be punctual and that siblings won't be annoying and pizza deliveries will come on time and that the roads will be traffic free.

One major solution to reduce our anger is therefore this: we must more regularly expect that bad things will happen to us. We must try to move as many of the items on the chart we just did from Column A (What makes me angry) to Column B (What makes me sad). We need to learn the art of being a bit gloomy about how things can turn out. Yes, plans do get changed, people do let you down sometimes, there are delays when you travel, and pizzas can arrive cold. These aren't nice things, but we should know that they are real possibilities, and aim not to be shocked by them.

The word 'pessimism' means expecting that, a lot of the time, unfortunate things will happen. Pessimism is frequently seen as the enemy of good things. People can be suspicious of dark thoughts. They believe it brings bad luck.

But, within reason, maybe it can be useful to warn yourself that some disappointments might come your way. Maybe your relatives won't be good at guessing what you want for your birthday. Maybe a friend might join another group at school. Maybe you won't do so well in an exam. These aren't welcome things, and maybe you can fight hard to correct them in the long term, but the important point for now is to realise that you have an option other than to get furious if they do unfold.

You could get a bit sad for a while, and then cheer yourself up by doing something silly and fun — like balancing a pile of books on your head or sliding along a polished floor in your socks — or, if you're particularly upset, by talking to someone you trust about what's bothering you. It's much better to share unpleasant thoughts than scream them at the top of your lungs or take them out on other people or objects.

CHAPTER 10

Anxiety

It's normal to feel anxious; that is, worried about how things are going to turn out. Our bodies have developed (during the process of evolution) to feel anxious quite a lot in order to protect us, especially from old-fashioned threats like angry animals (or angry people!). That's why our bodies do things like get sweaty palms, make our hearts beat fast, or make us feel a sharp kick in the pit of our stomach when we are scared. It is an old-fashioned response that is meant to help us be ready to fight back against threats, or else run away from them. When we feel these things we can feel grateful that our body is looking after us in the best way it knows how.

But today, many of the threats that we face look different. Maybe you get anxious about school work, or about going to a party, or about travelling to a new place. When you get anxious, people tend to say, 'Don't worry, everything is going to be fine.' They are being nice, but it doesn't always help that much.

Here's another way to cope with anxiety. Tell yourself that:

Whatever happens,
you will survive

So yes, maybe the exam won't go brilliantly. But you can survive. Or you'll feel a bit left out at the party; but you can survive. Or it might be a bit uncomfortable when you go on the school trip; but you will survive.

Trying to remind ourselves that we can survive belongs to a way of thinking called *resilience*. Resilience means being able to bounce back from things that go wrong.

Resilient people know that a human being can take a lot of knocks, and still carry on. It may not feel like it. It may seem that you'll break apart and shatter like glass, but you won't. We're all pretty tough creatures and have been throughout our history. We're not actually made of glass.

Now let's think about ships. In the 17th century, the Dutch developed a tradition of painting that depicted ships in violent storms. These works, which hung in private homes, in schools and in offices, were not just exciting to look at. The pictures were also trying to teach people a lesson about resilience. The ships looked in terrible trouble, but they weren't sinking; they were in the process of making it through a storm. The Dutch painter Ludolf Bakhuysen painted a very famous picture called *Warships in a Heavy Storm* in 1695.

This sturdy ship can survive the rough sea, just like humans can survive rough times

Ludolf Bakhuysen, *Warships in a Heavy Storm*, 1695

It looks like madness out there: surely the ships will sink. But they won't. Dutch ships were carefully built to survive the worst kind of storms. The ships had sleek, strong hulls and short, sturdy masts. The crews practised emergencies all the time and knew how to stay steady on top of gigantic waves. In a few hours, those ships were going to be safe in their harbour.

This isn't really about ships, it's about you. You too are a bit like a Dutch ship from the 17th century. You might look fragile and there are big waves out there sometimes, but you've been perfectly engineered to sail through the most astonishing troubles. Hopefully you won't have to go through too many, but if you do, whatever you fear, you will make it. The ship did — and you will too.

A lot of anxiety looks like this:

PART A

If X happens…

PART B

I won't be able to survive

Notice that there are two parts to that statement: A and B. Most of the time, when people are trying to calm us down, they focus on addressing Part A. They tell us that X, what we fear will happen, won't happen. This is meant kindly and it can sometimes work, but it doesn't properly help and, in the long run, it actually makes us more anxious. Because what if X does happen?

So it is better to focus on Part B, the feeling that you won't survive, and knock that on the head. Whenever you're anxious (maybe you have an exam, or you have to go somewhere on your own), look squarely at what you think you won't survive and realise that, in one way or another, you will. It might be pretty tough, and 'survival' might include you shedding a few tears, but you will get through it. Maybe there's some things you can do now that will help. Increasing your sense of resilience is vital to making yourself ready for life.

You are far stronger than you think; a lot could go wrong, and you'd still be OK. The way to be sure is to think it through. Often, we make the mistake of not thinking *enough* about things that make us anxious. We worry about them, and we tell them to go away, but we don't ask them any questions.

So an idea to stop ourselves from being tormented is to stare our troubles in the face. We could ask:

What's the worst
that would happen if...

Often, we find that the worst would not be ideal, but OK. We mustn't leave our fears to grow at the back of our minds. We need to bring them out in broad daylight and get to know them. Even better, we should chat them through with a friend who knows, in a way, about resilience, and ships that make it through storms.

CHAPTER 11

Confidence

All of us sometimes feel lacking in confidence. Maybe we have to start a new school, or give a talk in front of the class; maybe we are going to a friend's house for the first time.

There is a standard way in which people try to boost our confidence at these sorts of moments. They tell us something along the lines of: *you're clever; you are a lovely person; you're great; you're amazing!* That sounds pretty good, but it's not the best way to make anyone feel properly brave. The best way is to say something that sounds quite odd. But it works.

Instead of saying, 'You're amazing; you'll be amazing', (because maybe you won't this time!), we say: 'You're a bit of an idiot, but don't worry, everyone else is too. We're all idiots, so don't worry about messing up! Every human who ever lived was a bit of an idiot, and that is more than OK.' This isn't being rude — it's the best way to feel brave in the face of a challenge.

Let's think of a situation where you might not feel confident. You've been asked to play a ukulele solo in the school concert, and to sing along too. You don't want everyone looking at you and are worried that you'll forget everything once you're on the stage.

Or here's another one: you've been asked to show someone important around your school and tell them all about it. What if you forget everything about your school, or you don't say enough, and they don't think your school is much good?

Or you have started at a new football club. You can see all the children from your new school are having a good time together, but you don't feel confident to go up and chat to them.

At many moments of underconfidence, we're faced with two contrasting emotions: a *wish* and a *fear*. The *wish* is to seem *serious* to others and most importantly to oneself, by which we mean cool, in control and grown-up. And the *fear* is of seeming like an *idiot* to oneself and others, by which we mean stupid, babyish and a loser. You could put it like this:

WE WISH TO SEEM

Competent
Worldly
Adult
Self-contained
Elegant
Composed

WE FEAR WE ARE

Disgusting
Needy
Frail
Eccentric
Weird
A loser

The normal way that people suggest we become more confident is to try to resolve the wobble in favour of the wish. They try to reassure us that we are actually serious, elegant, composed, etc. What we are really not — these kindly people say — are idiots.

This is very well-meaning and kind. But we find it does not work. Let's take a different approach. Rather than saying that we are all amazing and great, we should make ourselves at peace with the thought that we are all idiots: you, everyone at school, everyone out in the street, everyone in the government, in fact, everyone everywhere pretty much at every moment.

Yes, all of us are twits. We have stupid thoughts, we bump into things, we forget stuff, we have weird habits, we fart, we look ridiculous, we have odd thoughts and dreams… In short:

We are all
absolutely daft

Strangely, this idea can help to give us confidence. If we know we might look stupid, because everyone does at one time or another, it gives us permission to try things where we risk looking stupid — which includes all the most interesting situations in life. If you are too concerned about looking sensible, you'll never audition for the school play, paint a crazy picture, or try speaking a foreign language.

Beneath the surface, we imagine that it might be possible to avoid being an idiot. But it isn't! It isn't possible to lead a good life without regularly making a complete idiot of ourselves.

What we need to do is to befriend our Inner Idiot. We all have one. You know it's there. Mostly you're desperate to stay away from the Inner Idiot. But please don't. Make friends with it. Get to know it in broad daylight. And be assured that everyone has an Inner Idiot too.

So tell yourself: you are an idiot; your mum and dad are idiots; and their mum and dad too… We all are. We've been idiots in the past, and we will be idiots again in the future — and that is just fine. That's what it means to be human.

Now for the good news: once we learn to see ourselves as idiots, it doesn't really matter if we do one more thing that might make us look stupid. The children we try to talk to could indeed think us ridiculous. The teacher running the school play might turn us down. But if they do, they're only telling us something we know already (remember that?): we're an idiot — and that's OK. We grow free to give things a go by accepting that being an idiot is normal. And every so often, things will go right: we make a friend, we get a part in the play, we learn a language...

So, next time you have to try something that might make you look like a fool, try what we at The School of Life call The Inner Idiot Exercise.

SAY ALOUD

I may blunder
I may look absurd
in the eyes of others
I may say something
out of turn
I may be unwanted
I may know no one
I may inadvertently shock
I may misread the situation
...
And on this basis I am human

Impostor syndrome

There are times when we are close to being able to do something fun and impressive. Perhaps we've been chosen for the top football team, asked to create a brilliant work of art or invited to join a cool club. And yet we find ourselves feeling so under-confident that we may turn down the chance. We don't take part because we are crippled by what is known as 'Impostor Syndrome'. This a belief that some people are OK doing stuff, but some people (us) are impostors; that is, people who are pretending.

THEY'RE LEGITIMATE BECAUSE
They seem confident
They seem sure
They seem error-free
They seem calm
They seem normal

I'M AN IMPOSTER BECAUSE
I doubt myself
I get anxious
I have weird thoughts
I make mistakes
I lose my temper

When we feel like impostors, we're bothered by the things that we know we do not do well but we can't see in other people. Without knowing it, we're dividing the world up into two camps: those of the Impostors and those of the OK or 'legitimate' (that means 'allowed'). We place ourselves with the Impostors because of the weaknesses we secretly know we have.

The problem with Impostor Syndrome is that we're too unfair to ourselves and too generous to other people. We assume that some other people are without errors and faults, and we use our errors and faults as arguments against ourselves.

But the truth is that even seemingly legitimate and important people have weaknesses and faults just like we do. Why is this so hard to believe? Because people don't tell us about their faults. We know ourselves from the inside, but we know others only from the outside. So we can only know about others from what they disclose. We are left to conclude that we are odder and weaker than everyone else. But, everyone is putting on a 'mask of success'. If we just go by what we publicly know, the mask-like exterior, we may feel that to be great at singing or football requires a level of invulnerability and strength we don't have.

Whenever you feel that you are an impostor, remind yourself that the impressive stranger is — despite the lack of surface evidence — just like you in all your weaknesses. There's no reason why you shouldn't succeed. We're all idiots and we're all a bit scared. Now go for it!

CHAPTER 12

Patience

It's easy to start thinking that people we know — our families and our friends — are annoying. When we think of them, all we can remember are the irritating things they do, like Mum's way of asking a million times if we have done our homework yet, Dad's way of telling long stories that he's already shared a hundred times before, your sister who does handstands in the kitchen when you're trying to finish homework, or your friend who explains in too much detail what he had for his last meal. On a bad day, you can end up thinking, 'Why are any of these people in my life?!'

On such a day, we have a useful exercise that can help you to calm down and rediscover patience — and a little bit of love too. This exercise is called The Weakness of Strength. It says that every strength that a person has will also bring with it a certain weakness — and every weakness will come with a particular strength.

When you feel fed up with someone who you basically like very much (but not at that moment), ask yourself:

What's the strong aspect of the weakness they are showing?

Of course, it's the weakness that will look largest, but the strength will be there too — if you just think about it for a moment.

It's a fact of life that every admirable side of someone brings with it some drawback or other. The fact that someone is strong and impressive in one area almost always means that they're weak and annoying in another way.

EXAMPLES OF WEAKNESSES AND STRENGTHS

WEAKNESS
Mum who nags

STRENGTH
Loving and reliable

WEAKNESS
Dad who tells stories

STRENGTH
Fascinating and curious

WEAKNESS
Sister's handstands

STRENGTH
A talented athlete

WEAKNESS
Friend who loves food

STRENGTH
Generous with snacks

TRY WRITING YOUR OWN

WEAKNESS

STRENGTH

WEAKNESS

STRENGTH

WEAKNESS

STRENGTH

WEAKNESS

STRENGTH

Here's something you can do the next time you feel you're losing patience with a friend or family member. Think about their good sides and then remember the probable weaknesses that go along with these strengths. Try writing your own examples in the table on the left.

This kind of table reminds us of a basic but always surprising fact:

There aren't any
perfect people out there

We're all made up of a huge number of strengths *and* weaknesses — and the two are linked. You couldn't be good at one thing without at some level being bad at something else. It's just the way it goes. And you? You're the same. You have a lot of great sides, but some bad ones too. People who love you always know that: they can see the link between your strengths and your weaknesses and they forgive you for the latter. Try it!

CHAPTER 13

Nature

We're often told that nature is good for us, that it's good to hang out with animals and to go out into the fields and forests. Mostly, when people tell us this, they're selling it to us on the basis of our physical health: getting a dog will help us get out more, going to the forest will mean filling our lungs with clean air... That's all true, but there's another benefit to nature too. Nature (by which we mean animals, as well as wide open spaces) is good for your mind.

The reason goes a bit like this: *nature doesn't care about you*. Nature does not mind how many followers you have on social media, who said what at school, when you will change class, who told on whom in front of the teacher, and all the many, many things that fill our minds and make us worry and anxious every day.

Take a sheep. A sheep knows nothing about you. It really does not care about what you're wearing or who your parents are. It's just busy being a sheep.

It's interested in eating, in sitting down somewhere comfortable and in keeping an eye on the rest of its flock. It may look at you a bit strangely, but frankly, it doesn't care about you.

Now that's a help. At last, you're in the company of a living being who just gets on and does its own thing — and it invites you to get on and do your thing without thinking too much or second guessing everything like we all often do. The sheep doesn't speak, but if it did, it might say something like, 'Just be calm like me, concentrate on the small things (like chewing) and let everything else take care of itself.' Dogs are a bit like this too, and cats, and pretty much any animal that won't eat you when it's hungry. You should hang out with them as often as you can — and leave your phone behind.

What about the rest of nature? Well, there's something calming about a big sky at dusk, when you can see the stars just starting to peek through. Or gigantic mountains, or the ocean from a cliff or the desert from an aeroplane. It's nice to be made to feel small in nature.

Normally, feeling small is a bad experience (when an enemy at school does it to you, for example), but when nature makes us feel small, it can feel cosy and calming. Nothing matters quite so much any more. We realise that we're all tiny, that there's a big universe that knows nothing about us, and that our problems aren't as vast as we sometimes think they are.

When we see the most impressive aspects of nature — distant mountain ranges; the sun going down behind massed banks of glowing clouds; huge waves pounding a rocky shore — in comparison with this, our own individual lives seem tiny and inconsequential.

At such moments, nature seems to be sending us a humbling message:

Accept what you cannot change...

...and don't worry so much about being you!

This sensation can be very comforting. Nature doesn't just make us look small, it makes our problems, our enemies and our heroes look small too. That helps.

Things that have up to now been looming large in our minds (what has gone wrong with the computer, the fact that a friend behaved coldly, the argument with our parents) tend to get cut down in size. Nature drags us away from the minor details that normally occupy our attention and makes us concentrate on what truly matters.

Nature is there to correct how we look at things — and that is why we should hang out with it. It helps us to be less worried about ourselves, less concerned with who we are and what we do and better able to see the big picture.

CHAPTER 14

The Adult World

To a 2-year-old, the idea of being 7 seems impossibly far away. The toddler knows that a 7-year-old goes to school and can read and understands lots of things, but the 2-year-old has little idea of what these things are really like. For a 7-year-old, the world of a 15-year-old seems remote and hard to imagine. But as you get older, you start to see more of the adult world. It's a strange mixture — in some ways it might look exciting; in other ways it can seem frightening or just mysterious.

In this section we're going to look at some of the ways you encounter the adult world.

Famous people

Some grown-ups are famous. Being famous sounds great: everyone has heard of you; you get paid a lot of money; lots of people would be excited to meet you; you can do exciting things. A lot of people want to be famous. That's tricky because hardly anyone actually is famous. Only one person out of every 10,000 is famous (if there are 500 children in your school, one person out of 20 schools like yours will be well known): that is an extremely small number.

But we could also ask: what might not be nice about being famous? Quite a lot of things. There's a lot of envy: people think your life is too nice, in comparison with theirs, and they might want things to go badly for you. If you make a mistake, everyone knows about it and lots of people laugh at you. You can't enjoy doing ordinary things, because people are always noticing you. If you want to have a quiet time you can't, because someone is taking a photo or tweeting about you. People say horrible things about you and you can't stop them. Mostly, a famous person has to work very,

very hard. And usually there was a long, difficult time when they were not at all famous.

Our idea of what it's like to be famous concentrates on certain moments: the crowd applauding, getting an award, making a speech. But we don't think so much of all the other things that go on in the background: the effort, the risks, the rejections, the hard negotiations, the criticism, and the insecurity.

Also, we don't hear anything about many, many people who are doing interesting things but are not at all famous. Fame is a first idea about what a nice life might be like. But it's not an accurate picture. Probably you shouldn't think too much about becoming famous one day.

The news

For a long time, when you were very little, people read you stories: maybe about a frog that became best friends with a mouse or about a princess who married a prince or a cat who jumped over a tree and landed on the moon. Everything worked out happily in the end.

Then, as you get older, you start to hear about the news. It's not a made-up story. Somewhere there was an earthquake; there's been a bomb in a city; people are fighting; something's going wrong with glaciers; there are lots of angry people in a street; people are arguing and getting upset about politics; there was a fire; someone had a knife and stabbed someone else. There are so many disasters and scary things in the news. It might be nice just to not pay any attention. But it's there at the back of your mind: maybe the world is horrible. It can make you feel small and powerless.

A good idea is to think about how news works. The news doesn't tell us *everything* that's happening in the world. It doesn't even tell us *a lot* about what's happening. It tells us very few things out of billions and billions of things that happen every day.

The news doesn't tell you about all the normal and quite OK (or really rather good) things that are happening everywhere. It just tells you about the things that went wrong.

If asked to comment on the scene on the previous page, the news would say something like: *today a very terrible thing happened — someone stole a biscuit!*

If that's all you heard, you would not get the full picture of what the day was like for these people. Lots of OK things happened as well, and plenty of nice things too. Only the news hasn't mentioned them. That's because the news doesn't tell you everything that happened; it only tells you the terrible things that happened.

The next time you're getting sad from reading the news, take a break and remember that this isn't the way the world is; it's just all the biscuits that have been stolen in the last 24 hours.

Jobs

One of the big differences between children and adults is that adults have jobs. Children go to school and grown-ups go to work.

Maybe you worry about what job you will do when you are a grown-up. Probably someone has asked you, 'What do you want to be when you are older?' and it can sound like a difficult and scary question. Maybe you don't know, but it sounds as if you are supposed to know.

WHAT IS A JOB?

An obvious thing about a job is that you get paid to do it. But behind that there's something that's not obvious at all: *why* do you get paid? A teacher gets paid to work at school, but you don't get paid for going to school. A professional tennis player gets paid for playing tennis, but millions of people play tennis without getting paid.

The explanation is that you get paid for helping someone else. A teacher helps you learn things; that's why they get paid. The tennis star helps you have an exciting time watching them play; that's why they get paid.

A job is really built around helping other people do things. That's why work can be enjoyable: we like feeling that we are being useful to other people. So the most interesting and enjoyable jobs are not necessarily the ones where you get paid most but where you have a clear and strong sense that you are helping other people.

There's a good way to start thinking about what you might do as a job. It's a bit surprising, because at first it doesn't seem linked to work at all.

The idea is to think about what you like doing. Quickly write a list of things you enjoy doing. It might be skateboarding, tidying your room, writing stories, taking the dog for a walk, going to a party... It could be anything. You might think this list is a guide to what jobs you might enjoy. If you like playing football, maybe you should be a professional football player; if you like sailing, maybe you should work on a ship. But it's more complicated than that.

Suppose you like writing stories. Someone might say: you should write novels when you grow up. It's an interesting suggestion, but maybe not a helpful one. Hardly anyone has a full-time career writing novels. In a fairly large country like the UK or France there might be 10,000 novels written each year. But only about 100 will make enough money for the writer to live on. That's one in a hundred. That means it's going to be very tough and involve a lot of luck.

So if you like writing, that's an interesting clue, but it's maybe not a *direct* guide to what to do for work. You can ask an interesting next question: *what do I like about writing?* Maybe you like making sense of other people. It could be that you really enjoy trying to explain things, or maybe you like having a lot of time on your own exploring your own ideas. These are all pleasures of writing, but they aren't *only* pleasures of writing. They could lead off in lots of different work directions. A travel consultant needs to understand people (the more they understand people, the better they are at their job, the more they can help others and the more satisfaction they get in the work). A manager in an office needs to do a lot of explaining, so people know what to do. So it's really helpful not just to stick with 'what I like' but to move to the trickier question:

What do I like about what I like?

Suppose you like basketball. You could ask yourself about the different enjoyable things that are connected to playing basketball. For instance, you might like being part of a team, or you might enjoy the way you can improve by practising. Maybe you like working out who the best players are and thinking about how they can work together to win. These are your 'underlying pleasures'. Normally you'd just say, 'I like basketball', but these are the special things about basketball that you especially enjoy.

Take a look at the table on the next page. On the left-hand side, write down the activities you enjoy. In the other column, say as much as you can about the underlying pleasures: the special things you enjoy about these things. It's quite tricky to do and it might take a long time, so don't worry if you can't finish it quickly. Once the question is in your mind you'll probably start to notice things and you can write them down later. We've filled in the examples we've just been talking about. The rest is for you.

The 'pleasures' don't tell you exactly what to do. But they can give you ideas. They suggest the kinds of things you might be spending time doing in a job that you find interesting and satisfying. The next time an adult asks you what you want to do when you grow up, tell them you are still thinking about it.

WHAT I LIKE

SPECIAL PLEASURES CONNECTED TO THIS

Writing stories

Understanding people; explaining things; working on my own

Playing basketball

Being in a team; improving a skill; helping people cooperate

TRY WRITING YOUR OWN

It doesn't make much sense to try to pick a future career early on. When you are 10 or 12 you can't really know what you want to do; a lot of people who are 22 or 32 don't know either.

One reason is that there are so many different kinds of jobs and it's hard to know what they are like. We tend to think mainly about obvious jobs like being a vet or a lawyer or starting a business developing an app. But what about being a logistics consultant or a safety engineer or a dental hygienist or a polling specialist or working in recruitment or designing the breakfast menu for a hotel? There are thousands of different kinds of jobs people do, but mostly you won't know what they involve or why they might be interesting or enjoyable.

It also means there might be a lot of different jobs you could enjoy doing. Working out what to do isn't really about discovering the one single thing in the whole world that's perfect for you. Rather it involves finding out the underlying kinds of things you enjoy doing and seeing where they match up with the different things people do for work. It may turn out that there are many overlaps. There might be quite a lot of different jobs you could enjoy doing and be good at.

You are not supposed to know right now. It does — and should — take a long time to work out where your personality best fits in terms of getting paid to help other people. If you've found out by the time you are 30 that would be amazing; most people take much longer than that.

Money

Grown-ups do talk a lot about money. Suppose that you ask, 'Is money important?' The odd and interesting thing is: there isn't a simple answer. Someone could have a lot of money and not be at all happy. If a grown-up has very little money that could be very hard — but there are plenty of people who don't have much money who really enjoy their lives.

Here's a way of thinking about money: it's like an ingredient in cooking. Let's imagine money is like sugar (you can have a lot of it or not very much) and you want to bake a cake.

If you have lots of sugar you might think: that's great, I can make a huge cake. But that's not really true. It depends on what other things you have. A big pile of sugar on its own won't help if you don't have any flour or eggs.

Even if you have very little sugar you can make something interesting — if you have other good ingredients. You could make some pancakes or a pizza (if you have some cheese).

In the same way, as an ingredient, money isn't much good on its own. The other ingredients for a good life aren't like money. They're to do with your thoughts and feelings and your personality. But if you have some of these other ingredients you can do a lot without much money. If you have a bit of money, you can also do good things if you have those other ingredients.

It's confusing because when people talk about money they don't usually remember that money is just one ingredient. They talk as if money is the only ingredient, but they've forgotten something that every cook knows.

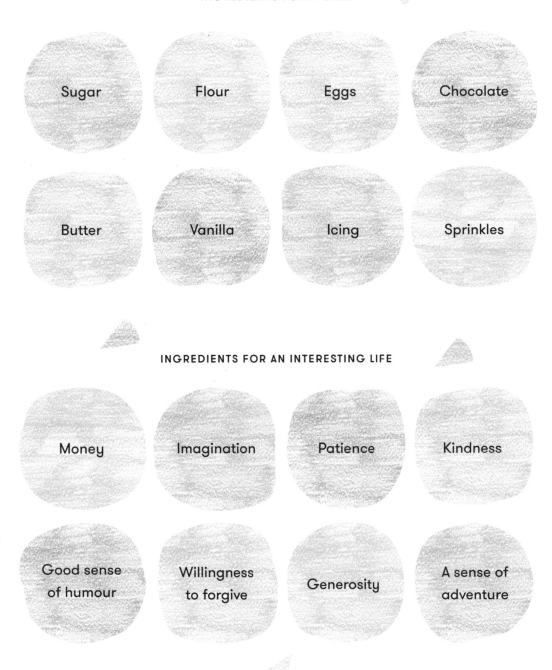

INGREDIENTS FOR A CAKE

Sugar

Flour

Eggs

Chocolate

Butter

Vanilla

Icing

Sprinkles

INGREDIENTS FOR AN INTERESTING LIFE

Money

Imagination

Patience

Kindness

Good sense
of humour

Willingness
to forgive

Generosity

A sense of
adventure

CHAPTER 15

Separation

When you are little, you can't imagine being independent of your parents. A 2-year-old needs their parents to help them put on a jumper or brush their teeth or to carry them if they get tired. At 10 you still need them a lot: they buy your food and clothes, they make sure you have somewhere to live and lots of other things. But, still, you are much more independent than you were when you were 2. You would probably find it annoying if a parent was still saying: 'Now, let's put this arm into your little jumper; that's good, now the other one. Oh, now your head is disappearing! Oh, there it is! Aren't you clever!'

In fifteen years' time, you might be sharing a flat with some friends or going off on holiday without your parents. You'll know how to get your own food and how to get a job and how to make some money and maybe how to drive a car and what to do at an airport. It will be up to you to get up in the morning and when you go to bed. That might sound scary now, but in fifteen years' time you will have gradually learned to do all these things and they won't feel scary at all.

Separation can sound sad, because it sounds as if you are abandoning your parents — or that they are abandoning you. But that is not really what's happening. You will be able to live apart from them quite happily; you'll still like them and feel close to them; you will still sometimes want their help or advice. Becoming more independent is a sign that things have gone well. You can look after yourself because you've been looked after well. It took a lot of work and a lot of love.

Finally, there is a very special idea that can help with understanding independence. It's got an odd name: *internalisation*. 'Internalisation' happens when someone else's intelligent and helpful thoughts become your intelligent and helpful thoughts.

Think of what happens when you learn to cross the road safely. At first you need a grown-up with you. They hold your hand, they say 'Stop here, look to one side, now look to the other, is there a car coming? Yes, there's a red car. We need to wait. Now it's clear (on both sides), it's safe. But we have to keep looking as we cross!' But gradually you learn to say these things to yourself. You are internalising your parent. You don't need them to actually be there with you to tell you because you have their voice in your head. Their voice, speaking in your head, keeps you safe, even though they are not physically with you.

It's the same with lots of things. For a long time, you need your parents to tell you when to go to bed. They say: 'You are tired, it's time for bed.' But eventually you'll be able to say this to yourself: you learn to say 'I'm tired, I think I'll go to bed.' You are *internalising* what a parent has told you so that eventually you don't need them to be there because a version of their voice is active in your mind.

Eventually, you will have internalised a parent enough so you don't need them to be there to help you. That's not because you do not care about them. It's for the opposite reason: you have *internalised* your parents' love and care, and you carry that about with you in your mind.

Even if you move to a different country when you are older, your parents will still be with you all the time in this special and important sense. You don't need to be physically together for your minds to be close. All the best things about them will be with you all the time, wherever you go.

59   Thomas Gainsborough, *Mr and Mrs William Hallett ('The Morning Walk')*, 1785. Oil on canvas, 236 cm × 179 cm. National Gallery, London.

77   Philip Galle, *A Painter's Workshop*, circa 1595. Engraving. Rijksmuseum, Amsterdam.

78   James Guthrie, *To Pastures New*, 1883. Oil on canvas, 92 cm × 152.3 cm. Aberdeen Art Gallery and Museums Collection, Aberdeen. Presented in 1888 by Francis Edmond.

79   Jan Steen, *The Village School*, circa 1670, Oil on canvas, 81.7 cm × 108.6 cm. Scottish National Gallery, Edinburgh. Purchased by Private Treaty with the aid of the National Heritage Memorial Fund 1984.

110   Portrait of Marilyn Monroe, May 1953. Hollywood, California. Photo by Alfred Eisenstaedt/The LIFE Picture Collection via Getty Images.

112t   Domenico Ghirlandaio, *Portrait of an Old Man and a Boy*, circa 1490. Tempera on poplar wood, 62.7 cm × 46.3 cm. Musée du Louvre, Paris.

112b   Rembrandt, *Hendrickje Stoffels (1626–1663)*, mid-1650s. Oil on canvas, 78.4 cm × 68.9 cm. Metropolitan Museum of Art, New York. Gift of Archer M. Huntington, in memory of his father, Collis Potter Huntington, 1926.

136   Ludolf Bakhuysen, *Warships During A Storm*, circa 1695. Oil on canvas, 150 cm × 227 cm. Rijksmuseum, Amsterdam. Purchased with support from the Rembrandt Association.

The School of Life tries to teach
you everything you need to have
a good life that they forget to
teach you at school. We have
shops all around the world,
we run a YouTube channel
and we have written a lot of
books specifically for younger
people, including books about
philosophy, art, architecture,
nature and the best way to have
a healthy and happy mind.

theschooloflife.com